"If you've always wanted to know more about investing in unit trust, this book is for you. Derek, being an industry practitioner since 2008, covers all that you need to know. I would strongly recommend the book to anyone who's keen to learn more about unit trusts!"

—Lim Wee Kiong, General Manager of iFAST Singapore

"Whenever someone asks me about investing in unit trust, I am very hesitant as there is not enough guidance out there on understanding and selecting the right unit trusts. But now, Derek has created a comprehensive guide on how individuals can understand and build a portfolio of unit trusts in a systematic and sound method."

— Sean Seah, Best-Selling Author of *Gone Fishing With Buffett*

"Derek's book on the theory and the practice of investing in unit trusts is an incredible tool for young people who want to start investing – *now*. It is truly one of the easiest means of building wealth over their lifetime. Take heed of the advice here and you will reap the rewards of intelligent investment!"

—Steven Lek, Founder, retiredowhat.com

"Derek is a great financial advisor whom I have built up a solid partnership with. He reviews my portfolio with me regularly and never forces his opinions on me. I am very excited that he has written this book, and would not hesitate to recommend him to other investors!"

—Mr Tan B. Y., Senior Manager, Sembcorp Design & Construction

Huat Ah!

Huat Ah!

Building Wealth in Singapore with Unit Trusts

Derek Gue

Singapore

© 2015 Derek Gue

Published by: Derek Gue

Website: www.derekgue.com

ISBN: 978-981-09-5489-5 (Paper)

National Library Board, Singapore Cataloguing-in-Publication Data

> Gue, Derek, 1982-
>
> Huat ah! : building wealth in Singapore with unit trusts / Derek Gue. – Singapore : Derek Gue, [2015]
>
> pages cm
>
> ISBN : 978-981-09-5489-5 (paperback)
>
> 1. Mutual funds – Singapore. 2. Investments – Singapore. I. Title.
>
> HG5750.67
>
> 332.6327 — dc23   OCN909000791

Front cover design by: Vesko, Intro Studios

Typeset by: Pressbooks

Printed by: Mainland Press

Distributed by: PMS Publisher Services Pte Ltd

Contents

PREFACE   ix

ACKNOWLEDGEMENTS   xii

INTRODUCTION   1

PART I. THEORY

1. Misperceptions of Unit Trusts   9

2. What are Unit Trusts   21

3. Why Buy Unit Trusts   36

4. Five Common Mistakes and Five Winning Tips   48

5. Emotional and Psychological States of Investors   67

    PART II. PRACTICE

6. How to Buy Unit Trusts   87

7. Where to Buy Unit Trusts   99

8. How to Read the Fund Factsheet, Product Highlight   108
    Sheet and Prospectus

9. Which Categories of Unit Trust to Buy   115

10. Factors that Affect Unit Trust Performance   145

    PART III. APPENDIX

11. Appendix 1: Good Questions to Ask Your FAR   161

12. Appendix 2: Interview with Wong Sui Jau   167
    Retirement Ambassador, iFAST Financial Ltd

13. Appendix 3: Interview with Apelles Poh   171
    Financial Advisory Branch Director

    Resources   181
    About the Author   183

PREFACE

I chose the title *Huat Ah! Building Wealth in Singapore with Unit Trusts* not to imply that you will become an instant millionaire by reading this book but to grab attention and evoke positive energy. "Huat Ah!" is echoed by many Chinese Singaporeans throughout the year, in Chinese weddings and especially during the 15 days of Chinese New Year. Moreover, the "U" and "T" in *Huat* is the abbreviation of unit trusts! This book strives to offer step-by-step advice to building your wealth with unit trusts, and act as your guiding compass in your journey to be financially free and independent.

Unit Trusts (UTs) have been available to Singapore investors for over 25 years and is one of the big five asset classes (together with stocks, bonds, structured products and insurance) that are sold by financial institutions in Singapore. There is approximately S$38.8 billion invested in UTs and managed by professionals as of end 2013. However there are only a handful of published books specific to the Singapore scene. The most recent one, *Investing in Unit Trusts in Singapore,* was published in 2000 by Peter Douglas and Andy Ong.

This publication in your hand updates the pool of research and offers the reader practical tips and insights on UT investment and managing your UT portfolio. It is for anyone who wants to find out more about Unit Trusts (UTs) in Singapore. Whether you have never invested before and this is the first investment book you are reading, or you are a seasoned investor and have a library of personal finance books, I am confident this book will provide you with invaluable information about this asset class.

As the backgrounds, ages and experiences of readers may be very diverse, I will include analogies, quotes, graphs and charts to bring to life flat and potentially confusing financial concepts. Technical terms will also be explained in brackets. At the end of each chapter, I summarise key learning points. For the experienced investors, please feel free to skip past such sections and read the parts of this book that you find most beneficial. For readers who have just started out on your investment journey, or this is the first few financial books you are reading, I suggest that you read one to two chapters a day instead of reading in one shot cover to cover. This way of reading will allow you to think about and absorb the contents of the book slowly, and will greatly increase your experience and learning from this book.

Most people work hard, and I believe their money should work as hard, if not harder! I also firmly believe everyone should enjoy their retirement years in happiness and not haplessness and regret because the banker or representative who sold them the financial products years ago did not do a good job. Neither should a regular investor that sets aside money for 18 years have to worry about their child's university education because of underperforming investments.

An area of work I find rewarding is orphaned accounts, which refers to situations where the banker or representative who sold UTs to the client has since left the organization and nobody is helping the client monitor his or her investments. This provokes anxiety as the client's capital is at risk. When disappointed clients, who had previously invested in underperforming UTs, transfer their UTs over to us, we give their portfolio a new lease of life and help them break even and see profits. The client's joy and relief expression becomes my greatest reward.

This publication is written from the perspective of a financial advisor who has advised over hundreds of clients and is managing a UT portfolio approaching S$3 million of investments at the point of writing. In my eight years (and counting) in the industry, I have experienced great satisfaction when I provide reviews and recommendations on client's insurance and investment portfolios.

These reasons gave me the motivation and courage to write this book and share my experience and opinions. I hope you will enjoy reading the book and be able to relate and apply some of the concepts and knowledge to gain the advantage for your UT portfolio that it fully deserved. Although you may not agree with 100% of material here but if reading this book deepens your understanding of Singapore UTs and made you a more knowledgeable and savvy UT investor, it would have served its purpose and make me very happy.

I will offer all readers a special bonus. If you email me, you will be able to attend a mini group discussion with me and other like-minded investors for free. This discussion, with hands-on activities like understanding a factsheet, UT highlight sheet, scenario analysis, etc., will be conducted every quarter or so. You can ask me questions on my book, current market conditions and if you bring your UT statements along, I will offer my views and recommendations on your portfolio. From the interaction, we can learn from other investors and from each other. Dates for the mini seminar will be posted from time to time on my website.

I welcome all comments or feedback on the book. You can email me at bwutbook@gmail.com or leave a comment on my website at www.derekgue.com. Thank you!

Derek Gue
May 2015

ACKNOWLEDGEMENTS

I'd like to thank the following people for making this book a reality. Firstly, I like to thank Mr Wong Sui Jau and Mr Apelles Poh for taking the time to be interviewed and for sharing their personal experience and nuggets of wisdom. I would also like to thank the people for their testimonials: Mr Lim Wee Kiong, Mr Sean Seah and Mr Steven Lek.

Also my editor Ms Christine Chong, for her invaluable dedication and hard work in rearranging the chapters in this book to give it better structure and flow as well as offering plenty of ideas to make this book more practical and beneficial to readers and investors.

A big thank you to all my clients who allow me into their lives as their trusted adviser for their Insurance and Unit Trust matters. By managing their unit trust portfolio over the years and hopefully many more decades to come, I have also gained tremendous practical knowledge and experience in unit trusts and the markets to share with everyone reading this book.

Special credit to my fiancée Grace, by leading from example through her successful book *Blogging for a Living*. Thank you for sowing the idea to write a book, and more importantly your companionship.

Lastly, I like to thank my parents for their unconditional love over the last 30 odd years.

INTRODUCTION

Do you know of anyone who has become a millionaire by putting his or her savings away in fixed deposits? Most people don't get rich this way. Millionaires know how to make some or even all of these 'M's to work for them: M – Money (They know how to grow their monies, have multiple streams of income or passive income, and invest wisely); M – Machines (They can be business owners and know how to invest in capital to produce more goods); M – Men (They know about human capital and who to employ and deploy to work for them); M – Methods (They know the steps and shortcuts in society and economy to play the 'money' game); and the last M – Motive (They have a strong motivation to become rich, whatever obstacles or distractions that may happen).

We need not all be millionaires to retire in Singapore, at least that is what the government tells us. However we will need to increase our financial quotient to put ourselves in the best possible position come that day. To give you an edge, I have sifted out a few golden rules, simple to understand, but takes discipline and hard work to follow. Cultivate these habits and they will be with you and serve you well for the rest of your life.

1. Wealth = Money x Time x Returns

Money = The more money the investor can save and invest, the more his/her wealth.

Time = The longer the time horizon or the earlier the investor starts and gets to compound his/her wealth, the more opportunities to profit from the market. Also with more time, investors will be able to gain better experience and a greater self understanding of his/her own investment style and risk appetite, etc.

Return = The higher the rate of returns, the faster the investor's wealth will grow.

2. Always pay yourself first

Do something today so the future you will be grateful to the present you. This principle can also be applied to other aspects of life (keeping fit, losing weight, other positive things that you wanted to do but always procrastinated doing).

3. Don't lose money

Buffett's first rule of investing. Assume you have $10 and suffered an investment loss of 10% in the first year. If in the second year, you make a gain of 10% of your balance at the end of the year 1, would you recover and break even? No, as you are still 10 cents short. Think about it: for every loss of 10%, you will need to make a gain of 11.11% on your remaining capital to recover. For every 20% loss, you will need to make 25% gain to recover. If the loss is 30%, the investor has to make 42.85% profit to recover the 30% loss. Remember Buffett's rule by heart as it is an important investment mantra.

4. Use financial gearing or leverage wisely

It is a double-edged sword that can multiply gains or losses rapidly. It is like using $1 of your own capital combined with borrowed funds to take up a $30 position (30x trading leverage). There will be costs of borrowing in using leverage. Always seek out deals with *positive leverage* where *underlying asset appreciates in value* > *borrowing costs*. An example is most properties purchased in Singapore with a mortgage loan in the last 30 years.

Excessive negative leverage in their debt to income levels in many US households brought about the 2008–09 global financial crisis. The problems in the real estate sector had a domino effect: the banks, which had a big exposure in the US real estate markets, had to write off many mortgage loans, causing banks to tighten their credit and loans books, which then further impacted other companies and industries as they found it difficult to obtain or extend their financing and faced liquidity problems. Employees were laid off, which compound the problem. Lehmann Brothers that went bankrupt during the crisis was found to have an accounting leverage of 30.7 times debt to assets.

Examples of other wealth instruments in Singapore

There are a ton of financial instruments to create and grow wealth in Singapore. On top of UTs, there are businesses, property, shares, structured products and, to a more limited extent, endowment insurance. Here is a general overview of UTs vs shares vs endowment insurance versus property in a table.

For business and structured products, it is hard to generalise and compare them as an asset class as they are so customisable and unique. Dual currency plans, equity linked notes, and structured notes are all examples of structured products that are widely marketed by banks in Singapore. UTs and shares are closer comparables as compared to property and endowment plans, which are separate asset class on their own. I decided to include them to give readers more information, since many Asians love to own a second property for rental income and capital appreciation especially in land scarce Singapore.

	UT	Shares	Endowment Insurance	Property
Pricing	End of the day. Forward pricing.	Buy real time price. Intraday.	Choose comfortable premium and premium term from onset.	As agreed between seller and buyer.
Contra	No	Yes. Settle after 2 days.	No	No
Decision on what to invest	Yes	Yes	No	Yes. Buyers can choose location and property type to invest.
Investment Amount	Min of $1,000 per UT and min of $100/ mth to invest.	In lot sizes of 1,000 shares. From Jan 19 2015, can buy lot size of 100 for some counter	Most endowment plans have a min of $50/ mth and min period of 10 years.	Usually a large investment depending on location.
Fees	Initial upfront fees. Platform and Wrap fees in some cases. Section 1.7	Charged by transaction. Approx $26.75 (online) or $42.80 (broker execute with GST)	Distribution costs goes to the insurance agents.	Stamp duties, valuation fees, agent fees, legal fees, other misc fees applicable
Voting rights	No	Yes	No	Yes, for strata titled properties.
Time needed to monitor(Ranking 1-Greatest,4 – least)	Yes. More time if online investing without representative. (2)	Yes. Greatly. (1)	No. Clients do not have control on participating fund investment (4)	Yes. More time if going to buy/sell. Not much for owner occupancy. (3)
Upon death	Deceased with will (Letter of Probate). Deceased without will (Letter of Administrator). Administrator's decision to sell units for proceeds or transfer holdings. Need death cert, administrator NRIC certified by lawyers.	Settle with Central Depository Pte Ltd (CDP). Need letter of administration or grant of probate. Need not sell can transfer to beneficiaries of deceased person's will or according to interstate succession act	According to nomination of beneficiaries under Insurance Act.	For Joint tenancy then 100% to surviving spouse. Otherwise according to the deceased's will, if not then interstate succession act.

Risk and volatility (1 – Greatest, 4 – least)	3. In my opinion, lower risk than shares and property as I have never heard of UT speculation vs shares/property speculation. Volatile due to world economy and outlook and factors listed in Chapter 10. Can always switch to bonds/low risk UT.	1. Company stocks are subject to business cycle and management risks, etc. Volatility can be reduced by holding a big portfolio of stocks of companies in different industries.	4. lowest risk as long as hold to maturity. There is guaranteed maturity sum added to non-guaranteed bonus based on mortality rates and insurance company's participating fund performance	2. Relatively high as seen from previous property boom and bust cycles in Singapore. Volatile prices due to economy's GDP, population growth, demand and supply of flats, interest rates, etc. When value of property drops significantly below outstanding loan amount, banks may request collateral or lump sum repayment

This book is narrow in subject matter and covers one investment class in great detail: unit trusts (UT) sold in Singapore. It is structured into two parts, with the first laying the theoretical ground work for a broad understanding of UTs and investing in general, and the second providing more detailed and practical advice for investors. Each chapter ends with learning points, and detailed explanations are provided in footnotes.

Part One begins with Chapter 1 exploring the misperceptions people have about UTs, this wonderful asset class. Chapter 2 explains what a UT is. Chapter 3 gives eleven reasons for investors to buy into UT. Chapter 4 lists a few common investment mistakes committed and a few tips on how to build a dream portfolio of UTs to get consistent positive returns. Chapter 5 will explore the 15 possible emotions as well as actions and practical tips, investors should be thinking during the investment cycle. We will use two fictitious characters (passive and proactive) and contrast their different thoughts and actions during the 15 stages. It concludes with what investors should consider before disposing of their investment(s).

Part Two begins with a discussion in Chapter 6 on Singapore's UT segment and where to buy UT; it also provides pros and cons between the different options. Chapter 7 suggests a few investment strategies that readers can use to invest in UTs. Chapter 8 will share with readers how to read the important documents of a UT: the fund factsheet, the UT product highlight sheet and also the prospectus. Chapter 9 will classify over 400 UTs for sale in Singapore into eight distinct categories. I will give a description of each category, their top holdings, and some performance ratios as well as my opinions on them. I will sift out two to three UTs within each category to analyse deeper with charts and finally the chapter will conclude with combining one UT from each category earlier in separate charts over different time periods to share some lessons that we can apply to our real life UT portfolio. Finally, in Chapter 10, I will share the economic as well as non-economic risks that will affect the performance of UTs; this allows readers to tell when an inferno is burning just from seeing the smoke from afar. They will be better able to make adjustments to their UT portfolio in future after reading this chapter.

There are three very practical and useful appendices. The first appendix will list good questions whenever you engage a Financial Adviser Representative (FAR). The second and third appendix are interviews with two people very heavily involved in the Singapore UT landscape and their opinions and thoughts on Singapore UTs in the next five to ten years. The first interviewee is Mr Wong Sui Jau, retirement ambassador in iFAST, the only listed UT platform company in Singapore. The second is Mr Apelles Poh, a branch director in a Financial Advisory firm and one of the most successful FARs in Singapore.

Endnotes

1. Contra means to offset. It was a popular strategy in the past for investors to buy the company share in the morning without paying any cash and sell the same security within the same day before market close. Because cash is only required at settlement date, two days after the trade is placed. As the investor has already sold his/her shares by then, the brokerage will contra/ net off and pay investor the difference.

PART 1

Theory

Misperceptions of Unit Trusts

Today, anyone can do a quick internet search for "Unit Trusts" (UT) and thousands of hits will appear. However, not all information on the internet is reliable, and there are many half-truths about investing in UT. Like every financial product, UT has its fair share of supporters and naysayers. In this chapter, I clarify some of the common misperceptions, some from the internet and general public and others from experienced UT investors, and offer the other side of the coin for you to consider.

1.1 Most actively managed UTs underperform the broad market

Many investors read on websites that it is better to invest in passive Exchange Traded Funds (ETFs) that are traded like a security on the exchange and track an index, a commodity, or a basket of funds. ETFs may have lower costs, but is it true that majority of them outperformed actively managed UTs?

Let's use some real-life examples to address this perception. There are over 30 different ETFs in Singapore, one of which is the Lyxor ETF Morgan Stanley Composite Index (MSCI) Emerging Markets, which tracks the MSCI Emerging Markets Index. Since ETFs track indices, outperformance is very rare due to tracking errors and the ETF manager's fees and other costs. I compare the MSCI Emerging Market index against four other active managed UTs that also invest in emerging markets in USD.

The charts below show that for returns over the last ten years and five years, the index underperformed all the four actively managed UTs. It is important to view the UTs and Indices and ETFs in the same chart before jumping to conclusions.

Fund Name	Annualised Returns	3 yr Annualised Volatility	Min NAV (SGD)	Max NAV (SGD)	Current NAV (SGD)
MSCI Emerging Market Index	3.71%	13.97	652.464	1944.424	1336.931 (23/02/2015)
Aberdeen Global Emerging Markets USD	5.35%	13.91	1.326	3.331	3.262 (23/02/2015)
JPM Emerging Markets Equity A (dist) USD	5.94%	13.38	20.429	54.834	42.179 (23/02/2015)
JPM Emerging Markets Opp A (Acc) USD	5.47%	12.95	133.522	410.925	323.449 (23/02/2015)
RJC Emerging Markets Eqty CJ USD	6.08%	13.33	29.798	79.717	87.313 (23/02/2015)

Fund Name	Annualised Returns	3 yr Annualised Volatility	Min NAV (SGD)	Max NAV (SGD)	Current NAV (SGD)
MSCI Emerging Market Index	0.17%	13.97	1090.228	1520.442	1336.931 (23/02/2015)
Aberdeen Global Emerging Markets USD	5.38%	13.91	2.437	3.331	3.262 (23/02/2015)
JPM Emerging Markets Equity A (dist) USD	2.07%	13.38	31.701	43.892	42.179 (23/02/2015)
JPM Emerging Markets Opp A (Acc) USD	4.48%	12.95	237.410	326.392	323.449 (23/02/2015)
RJC Emerging Markets Eqty CJ USD	3.07%	13.33	50.261	69.307	87.313 (23/02/2015)

It may be true many actively managed UTs perform poorer than ETFs that track indices. However from this example and later for STI ETF (section 9.6), there are still quite a number of actively managed UTs that consistently outperform ETFs and indices they are benchmarking for periods of ten years. Darwin's survival of the fittest prevails and UTs that consistently deliver sub-par performance or are poorly managed will eventually be weeded out; as there will be more fund outflows than inflows, eventually the UT's fund size becomes so small that it is not viable to continue operating.

UTs with a track record of over ten years usually continue to flourish; their fund managers and teams deserve credit for continuing to evolve their investment styles and methodology to adapt to changing dynamic market cycles and demands. These UTs with long track records of beating ETFs and the index they benchmark may grow bigger in fund size due to funds inflow from termination of competitor UTs, resulting in lower expense and fees for the investor. My opinion is that actively managed UTs, especially those with a track record of over ten years, stand a good chance of outperforming ETFs. The charts show the net returns after deducting the fund manager's fees.

1.2 High UT fees reduces profit and increases loss

The upfront fees, annual management fees and other applicable fees (wrap fees, platform fees and performance watermark) discussed in section 2.7 are all costs to the investor and will certainly reduce his/her net profits. If costs are the greatest concern to the investor, he/she should buy UTs online, instead of meeting up with a representative of the distributor. He/she should also buy UTs that track the indices.

Lion Global Investors acts as the representative local fund manager[2] and currently has three UTs in Singapore that track the indices: Infinity European Stock Index, Infinity Global Stock Index and Infinity US 500 stock index. These three UTs are passively managed and feed into the Vanguard European Stock Index fund (tracks the MSCI Europe Index), Vanguard Global Stock Index fund (tracks the MSCI World Free Index) and Vanguard US 500 Stock Index Fund (tracks the Standard & Poor's 500) respectively. These three UTs from the Vanguard Group track and replicate the index and will thus have lower costs, compared to their active fund manager counterparts. Almost all UTs in Singapore are actively managed, making the three Infinity UTs the minority.

Most investors will not mind paying higher fees as long as the performance justifies it. An analogy can be found with gym users: there are always clients who would rather pay more to get a personal trainer to motivate and structure the training to see faster results. Buying UTs through a representative or actively managed UTs certainly entails higher upfront fees compared to the online purchase of UT and passively managed ETFs. However, UTs are not long-term commitments compared to insurance plans and if after two or three years, the investor feels there is little benefit or the services of the rep does not meet expectations, he or she can easily transfer the holdings out to another platform with lower fees or to another rep to manage.

1.3 UT returns are too slow and too little

Most UTs hold over 30 securities/companies; this obviously leads to slower returns than individual stocks. However, as a result of holding many companies diversified across different sectors of the economy, *most UTs drop less dramatically than individual stocks during a recession.* Better managed UTs may drop less than their benchmark and their reference index.

That UT returns are slow and too little is not entirely wrong. This is because, unlike other wealth instruments like FX (currency), shares, etc., it is not possible to use leverage, margin trading or contra to invest in UTs in Singapore. The investor must pay the upfront sales charges in full to invest in Singapore UT, only when the monies are cleared can the fund manager make purchases. This makes UT less 'sexy' and more suitable for a medium-term investment of at least three years. However I have never heard of anyone in Singapore going into debt, becoming bankrupt or even committing suicide because of UT investments.

Investing in UT is boring; it hardly gives investors 5% returns in a single day, less common of 15% in a single week and rarely do any UTs in Singapore suffer a heavy sell off and see the NAV drop over 50% in a single month. However, George Soros once said: "If investing is entertaining, if you're having fun, you're probably not making any money. Good investing is boring." The investor needs to be conscious of whether he/she is investing or speculating.

Many investors remember the Singapore penny stock crash saga in Oct 2013 when the share price of Blumont, Asiasons and LionGold tumbled almost 90% in a week, because of Blumont's management's inability to satisfy SGX enquiry of how they grew their market value over ten times in just 13 months. Blumont shares used to be 2 cents a share, with a single lot (1,000 shares) costing $200 in Mar 2012. On 1 Oct 2013, before the speculative bubble burst, it was $2.50 a share, and a single lot would cost $2,500 (an amazing growth of 12.5 times or doubling investors monies 3.5 times in only 1.5 years). Blumont's share closed at 1.9 cents on 24 Dec 2014 and investors were back to square one. Greedy speculative investors with a punting mentality who bought many lots at $2 and held on are still badly burnt even after a year. The gains from shares, especially penny stocks, can be very fast and tempting and is even more dangerous if leverage is used.

1.4 Fund managers are restricted by the UT's investment objectives

The main criticism of traditional UTs is that fund managers must keep to the investment objectives even during recessions. For example, they have to stay invested even when the price of their companies free fall, cannot sell out, and are mostly not allowed to hold >10% in cash any point of time. The fund manager has to adhere strictly to the investment mandate and objectives at all time, otherwise the trustee has to report it to the regulators. There are two sides to every coin and the good thing about UT fund managers having to walk a tight rope and constantly being supervised by the trustee with regular audits is that it safeguards investor monies; otherwise many of the fund managers will have absolute power and liberty to invest in any company they desire. This certainly sounds like a red flag and investors better stay clear of unregulated/low supervision investments.

To circumvent this restriction, the investor can first take advantage of the free switching offered by the wrap account or fund switching that all UT platforms have and switch out to Money Market (MM) or short duration high grade bond UT. MM UTs are known to preserve value and maintain high liquidity to give returns on par with SGD deposits. The investor can switch out of equity UTs entirely into MM UTs at any time to take shelter before or in the early days of the recession.

The other way to address this concern is to own a diversified portfolio of UTs with investment mandates that give the fund managers more room to invest so long as they maximise total returns in the long run. The investor will have to look carefully at the UT factsheet and study the UT objectives and holdings well, or they can consult their reps. An example is the Hedge Fund UT that can make money for the investor even in a bearish market (Man AHL SGD Trend). Another example is a multi-asset UT like (Blackrock Global Allocation fund), where the investment objectives states there is no prescribed limits to the percentage of equities to bonds that the fund can hold as they adopt a flexible investment style. An observation about this UT as at end of July 2014, they were holding 23.2% of the total fund size of US$22 million in cash, an uncommonly high percentage for most Singapore UTs. Thus investors who want their monies to be managed by fund managers with greater autonomy with a more flexible mandate can choose UTs like the Blackrock Global Allocation fund.

1.5 Investors should buy only award-winning UTs

Awards for UT performance or being in the top quartile of its peers are usually given out before individuals invest and thus may already have been reflected in their NAV. Such fund managers may be treated like superstars and may even be poached to join other fund houses. John C. Bogle in his book *Common Sense on Mutual Funds* (1999) states that the average superstar fund manager limits their association with a given fund and their average tenure at the helm lasts only five years. Therefore investors should try and find out who the current fund manager of the UT is and whether the awards were won by this fund manager or by the ex-manager that has since left.

Many UT factsheets will list the awards their UT had won,

were given by Morningstar, Lipper or other fund rating agencies. As the editors of the Morningstar Mutual Funds have admitted, their star ratings are not strong predictions of future values and performance. It does not mean that 5-star funds will perform better than 4- and 3-star funds going forward.

However there is a strong history of 4- and 5-star rated UTs outperforming their 1- and 2-star peers if held over time. A UT's star ratings may drop not necessarily due to its poorer performance but due to new changes in the judging criteria, UTs changing their classification category, new UTs created or closed, etc. Thus investors should use the Morningstar ratings and awards as a gauge; if their holding period is long, then it is better to select UTs with higher star ratings and monitor those instead of investing in lower rated UTs and hoping for a turnaround.

1.6 Investors should buy UTs with bigger fund sizes

People tend to equate having more and being bigger as being more successful, for example, restaurants with more outlets must be more popular and have better food. However, does this hold true in the investing world? For big fund size UTs, with billions in Asset Under Management (AUM), there may be benefits associated with economies of scale, such as sharing of management fees, transactions costs, opportunities especially for bigger bond fund UTs (where certain MNCs or countries will prefer to borrow $500 million from one source versus $100 million from five different sources).

The question of whether a fund is big in its size is relative to the investment objectives and style of that particular UT. Some UTs investing in large cap companies (companies with a net market value above US$1 billion) may function better if they have a bigger fund size whereas UTs that specialise in buying small and medium cap companies may see performance suffer by having too big a fund size.

To give an example, two UT fund managers, one managing $100 million AUM and the other managing $500 million AUM, both decided to invest 10% of their AUM in a certain company. The fund manager about to invest $50 million may face more problems because the market value of small and medium cap companies is smaller, meaning $50 million will be more likely than $10 million to drive up the share price and create speculative problems. Fund managers with bigger AUM investing in smaller and medium cap companies will thus have little choice but to spread their investments across more companies, some of which may not exactly be among the manager's first choice. The UT managers will also not want to buy too much equity in single small-mid cap companies, which may result in them having a controlling stake, and hence management responsibilities, in the company.

Being small can be beautiful too, as fund managers can be more nimble and can afford to be more selective in buying companies as their resources are limited. For example, take Warren Buffett, who first started Buffett Associates Ltd with six other investors and approximately US$105,000 capital in May 1956. The first 20 years saw phenomenal growth of those pioneer investors' funds. He famously lamented in 1999 that he could generate higher annualised returns if only he had lesser monies (he coined it the "fat wallet challenge").

It is good to look at current fund size of the UT before investing and investors should be more concerned if there is a change in either direction of the fund size. Too rapid a drop in fund size would get the attention of most investors as it could signal an impending recession, or outflow to a competitor UT. Fewer investors are aware that too rapid a growth in fund size could spell trouble as well, especially for UTs with objectives that invest in small to medium companies as it may cause performance to be diluted.

More investment funds will pour in rapidly when the UT receives awards or gets mentioned by renowned analysts. Distributors will tell its sales force to sell that particular UT. This may cause the best years of the UT to be behind them and could be a signal for investors to switch to another UT because managing $20 million and aiming for a 6% annualized growth is certainly easier compared to managing $200 million and expecting the entire $200 million to also grow at 6%. Therefore, it is not size that matters but if the fund size is optimal for the category and investment style of UT; volatile investment inflows and outflows in their fund size may in fact disrupt the strategy of the fund manager. Hence big or small size funds have pros and cons, and it is more important for investors to keep a lookout, identify and monitor the UT's fund size closely every two to three months.

1.7 Investors should rush to invest before ex-dividends date[4]

Salespeople are often eager to get their clients to sign on the dotted line and quickly purchase UTs, especially if the UT has quarterly or annual dividend payouts. For example, Eastspring Investment MIP Class A payouts $0.05 per unit on the first working day in Feb every year, based on the current NAV of $1.036/unit (Sept 24, 2014); the dividend is equivalent to approx 4.68% assuming 3% upfront sales charge.

I studied this fund's NAV on the final day of the Ex date and on the next trading day after the Ex date from its first dividend payout in Feb 2006 right until Feb 2014 (Table below). Therefore I conclude that there is *no* difference in the investor buying UTs just before the Ex date or after. The NAV of the fund will drop by the same corresponding amount as dividends will be paid out from cash of the UT; once the dividends have been paid out, the UT's cash drops, so does the UT's NAV per unit. To the best of my knowledge, this is also true for all other dividend paying UTs.

	Final day Ex date	One day after Ex date	% Drop after ex date
1st div payout	27 Jan 06 (1.05)	1 Feb 06 (1.002)	4.571
2nd div payout	31 Jan 07 (1.081)	1 Feb 07 (1.034)	4.347
3rd div payout	31 Jan 08 (1.063)	1 Feb 08 (1.009)	5.079
4th div payout	30 Jan 09 (0.816)	2 Feb 09 (0.768)	5.882
5th div payout	29 Jan 10 (0.995)	1 Feb 10 (0.946)	4.924
6th div payout	31 Jan 11 (1.05)	1 Feb 11 (1.001)	4.666
7th div payout	31 Jan 12 (1.038)	1 Feb 12 (0.989)	4.721
8th div payout	31 Jan 13 (1.108)	1 Feb 13 (1.056)	4.693
9th div payout	30 Jan 14 (1.04)	3 Feb 14 (0.99)	4.807

1.8 UTs are always cheaper and more value for money at launch

Many investors ask me if they should buy new UTs at launch. I advise them to wait at least two to three months for the fund house to produce their first fund factsheet. Without this, investors do not have factual information on the UT's top 10 holdings, track record and fund size, meaning they will not know the expense ratio, etc.

UT new launches are *different* from a company IPO (Initial Public Offering) because, unlike IPOs of companies where the number of ordinary shares to be offered is fixed as the valuation of the company was already done, UTs can issue an indefinite number of new units. Therefore it is rare and almost impossible for a new UT launch's NAV/unit to rise to a premium on the first day, regardless of the buying or selling activity and level of over or under subscription to push up/down the NAV/unit. In Sept 2014, the Ali Baba IPO closed higher by 38% at the end of its first trading day but I do not think many UTs will even close higher by 3.8% at the end of its first full week of inception. At the end of the first day, the UT portfolio is represented as 100% cash with no securities to have an appreciation in the NAV; moreover there are costs for the launch, management fees, etc.

There are pre-launch costs most UTs have to incur: marketing and advertising campaign to broadcast their launch, legal and regulation costs, printing costs, etc. These costs can exceed a few million dollars, which is amortised over a period of time as expenses of the UT and invariably will reduce the NAV/unit.

Another reason against buying new UTs at launch is that they are probably overpriced. Most new UTs are launched when markets are bullish on that particular theme or sector or region. It is easier to launch and market a UT at a time when the investment objective is 'hot' and 'in' so response to the launch will be good and the fund manager can raise more funds. This also means that the prices of the underlying companies in the UT holdings are more expensive since it is a bull market and these are current flavours of the market.

If the UT raised a big capital as its initial fund size, it may lead to bigger problems because most fund managers are restricted by the mandate to hold under 10% of the fund size in cash. Therefore he/she has to invest the initial large sum of cash in a rising market to purchase the companies, which at present could be overvalued especially if the UT was launched near to the peak of its market cycle.

Lastly, do not invest just because of the sales charge discount or vouchers that the distributor or the fund managers usually offer for newly launch UTs. Look at the fundamental objectives of the UT as well as look through the prospectus and background of the fund managers. The investor can proceed to invest if he has done all the research and feels that the UT launch is only at the start or middle of the recovery phase, and there is still plenty of future upside to the NAV of the fund, coupled with the promotions and other savings at launch.

Key learning points

- It may be true many UTs underperform the broad market over prolonged period and hence it is better to buy ETFs with lower costs, but there are also many award-winning UTs with good fund managers. The key is in knowing how to find them using charts and other comparison ratios.

- In a crisis and free falling markets, even though most UT managers cannot hold 100% cash, investors can outright sell, switch to cash fund or choose a fund that gives the manager a flexible investment mandate.

- Unlike trading, UTs are for medium- to long-term investments thus returns may seem slow and too little for some. But we know in the tortoise and hare race, the tortoise wins eventually. I see trading more as a sprint, and investing more as a marathon.

- Investors can use the awards and the star ratings of the UT as a gauge but should not be the absolute criteria in their selection.

- Optimal fund size for UTs based on its own investment objectives will help the fund manager to invest and manage more efficiently (e.g., bigger fund size for UTs investing in big cap companies and smaller fund size for UTs investing in small cap). Investors should also be watchful of performance if fund size grows too fast or drops too much.

- All else constant, there is no difference between buying UTs on ex-dividend date or immediately after dividend date (xD date)

- If possible, avoid buying newly launched UTs with no track record. Ideally, wait at least six months or longer for more clarity and a portion of launch costs might have been accounted for.

Endnotes

2. Lion Global Investors mirrors the three UTs started by the Vanguard Group: the Vanguard European, Vanguard Global and Vanguard US 500. They cannot use the Vanguard name hence they use Infinity to market these UTs in Singapore through Lion Global Investors, which is a fund house that also manages other funds. These three funds passively replicate the Vanguard funds holdings and transactions; when the latter buy/sell securities, Infinity will follow as closely as possible.
3. Refers to the cut-off date that investors must be invested in the UT to be entitled to the dividends. It can be annual, quarterly or monthly depending on the dividend distribution.

What are Unit Trusts

2.1 Origins of Unit Trusts (UT)

Mr Ian Fairbairn was widely credited with starting the world's first unit trust in 1931. He wanted to model United States (US) mutual funds, which he noted were more resilient during the 1929 Great Depression, and also felt that the people of the UK should have more ownership of big local companies.

A UT is also known as a collective investment scheme (CIS) that pools the monies of investors, who select the particular UT with investment objectives they are most optimistic in and feel will represent the most probable chance of appreciating. This pool of money is professionally managed by the fund manager and his/her team.

2.2 Mutual Funds versus Unit Trusts

Mutual funds, as they are commonly known in the US, share many similarities with UTs (the term used in most Commonwealth countries). These two terms are often used interchangeably. Some slight differences are:

- UT generally follows an investment strategy to buy and hold. Mutual funds will often adopt an active trading strategy.

Usually UTs holds fewer securities (a share of a public listed company) than a mutual fund.

- A newly launched UT will issue a fixed number of units to build up fund size and grab the investors' attention. A mutual fund can create more new units when demand is greater, thus they can have literally an unlimited number of shares available to trade.

Since this book caters more to Singapore and Malaysia readers/investors interested in Singapore UTs, we will use the term "UT" and not "mutual funds".

2.3 Unit Trust's name and investment objective

Firstly, all UTs in Singapore have a fund name and an investment objective. The fund name will give potential investors a snapshot of the fund's *where* (geographical allocation of the investments or specific sector of the economy) and *what* (their holdings, whether it is investing in equities or bonds, or a hybrid of both etc.).

If the fund's name interests you, go on and explore the *how* by reading the fund's objective. It is usually written in a simple manner to describe and further add on the *where*, *what* and *how* this fund invests. How; will give you an idea of the strategies used by the fund managers to manage and grow the investments. After understanding the 2Ws (what and where) and the 1H (how) better, there could still be 3 more common Ws in the mind of the investor. (**W**hy should I invest? and **W**hen and **W**ays to invest in UT will be touched on in later chapters.)

The fund objectives/mandate can thus be said to resemble the rules in games and sports, so all parties are clear of the basic do and don'ts. Imagine a soccer or basketball game without rules!

If you neither understand, nor like or feel there is an opportunity for your capital to appreciate after reading the fund objective, do not invest in this particular fund. Seek clarification and advice from your financial advisor representative (FAR) or go ahead and look at other UTs. There are over 400 to choose from in Singapore!

2.4 Structure of a Unit Trust and the role of the parties involved

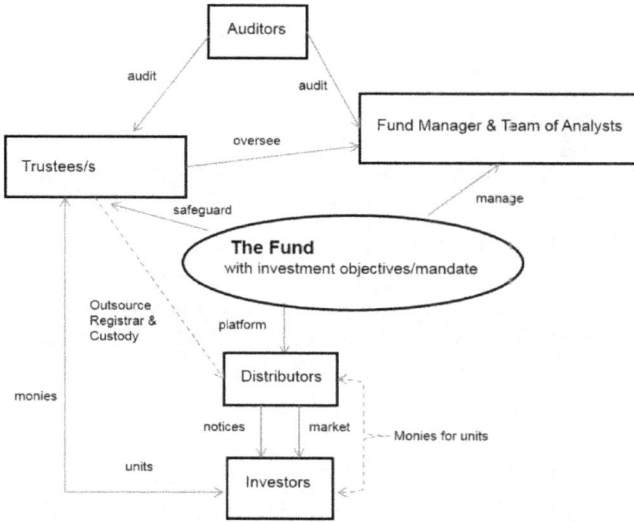

2.4.1 Fund Manager

An individual employed by a fund house to make day-to-day investment decisions on behalf of the collective group of investors. He or she also conducts site visits to potential companies they want to invest in, and meets up with their management team to understand their operations and financial books better.

Funds with bigger assets under management (AUM) or funds with global asset allocation may have several fund managers situated in different continents to improve their exposure and recommend the adding of new companies or increasing the percentage holdings of the present company. In a multi-fund manager UT, there is a lead fund manager who makes the final decision; together, fund managers hold regular video conference calls to discuss and coordinate their investment strategy.

The fund manager works for a fund house and is supported by a team of investment and research analysts who perform quantitative analyses. Most UTs have computerised systems with built-in formulas and parameters that execute trades when certain triggers and price points are met, hence they are able to put through hundreds or even thousands of trades in a day.

The fund manager's role is thus like the captain of a ship: he or she makes investment decisions on behalf of the investors.

2.4.2 Trustee

Usually a financial institution (banks or insurance companies) that holds the legal title and holds in custody all the assets of the fund. The assets comprise the cash from new subscriptions, the holdings of the fund, and monies that have yet to be invested. The Trustee can pass on the custody and registrar duties to another independent firm if they do not wish to be tied down with too much administrative work. Some Trustees delegate these functions to the Distributor (dashed arrow).

The Trustee also safeguards the investors' interest and ensures the fund manager is investing the assets according to the fund's investment objectives. The Trustee has the power to appoint another fund manager to replace the current fund manager if he is found investing against the fund's objective, becomes insolvent, or if a majority of the voters vote against him. The Trustee is also required by most Regulators to report major deviations or irregularities to the relevant authorities.

The role of Trustee in a UT structure is like an overseer or an independent marine authority: check and ensure that the captain stays on course with the help of the radar and other instruments (e.g., having auditors to ensure compliance by the fund managers).

2.4.3 Distributors

Responsible for marketing UTs to the masses and institutions, some distributors also take on a custody and registrar role from the Trustees for a fee. If they take on the registrar role, they will need to send fund house and fund manager's notices and other necessary reports to comply with regulatory requirements to notify investors. If they take on the custodian role, they will need to mail out dividend cheques to the investors or other payouts announced by the fund manager. There are two main types of distribution channels.

- Online: For example, Fundsupermart
- Face-to-face: Brick and mortar (banks and insurance companies) or a distributor that partners financial advisors to market unit trust (iFAST). Some fund houses are also distributors of their own funds and sell funds directly.

Distributors are like (tour agencies) that help to market the fund house and fund manager (cruise company) and match the fund's investment objectives and features (itinerary) to potential investors (clients).

2.4.4 Investors

Individuals or groups that had given or invested their monies in exchange for units in the trust. They will have a direct stake in the performance of the unit trust: if the price of the units goes up, the value of their investments will appreciate, and the reverse is also true.

The investors are like passengers on the cruise ship sailing on their journey towards financial freedom. They have the power to choose their preferred cruise and captain (fund house and manager), their preferred itinerary (investment objectives), which tour agency they want to sign up with (distributor) and also importantly when they will like to exit the cruise (fully sell off their investments), or upgrade their cabin or extend the duration of their cruise (increase their unit holdings in that UT).

2.5 Types of Unit Trust and common terminology

2.5.1 Offshore vs Onshore

Offshore UTs are incorporated and registered in a foreign country, usually low tax jurisdictions like Isle of Man, Jersey, Luxembourg, etc. Offshore UTs approved for sale in Singapore are known as "recognised funds"; they form the majority of the UTs sold locally. Onshore UTs are UTs incorporated and sold within the same country.

2.5.2 Open-ended vs Close-ended

Open-ended funds can create new units to meet future demand, and investors can buy more units anytime. Close-ended funds usually have a fixed number of shares and new units will not be created, thus investors may not easily buy more units or increase their investments after a stated closing date. Over 90% of UTs sold in Singapore are open-ended.

2.5.3 Capital Guaranteed vs Capital Protected

A small percentage of UTs marketed for sale in Singapore has capital guaranteed or capital protected feature, meaning the investor receives a fixed amount of money at the end of the investment term. These UTs are also sometimes candidly referred to as 'airbag' funds; like airbags in cars, they give a certain degree of protection and insurance.

To insure this return, the fund manager usually uses a portion (approximately 60% to 70%) of the investor's monies upfront to purchase long duration bonds that can have eight to ten years tenure. These lower risk long duration bonds will return the principal with interest upon maturity, so after eight to ten years depending on the initial structure, as long as the investor holds the UT until the end of the pre-determined tenure, he or she will be getting the initial invested amount back less the sales charges. Note, most guarantees on capital guaranteed and capital protected funds *do not* cover the sales charges. A bank or financial institution will usally provide the guarantee as long as it does not go bankrupt during the period of the guarantee.

Capital protected funds also use a portfolio of bonds to provide the airbag. The difference is that capital protected funds usually will not guarantee the full amount of the initial invested capital. Although capital guaranteed UTs are able to provide stronger assurance than capital protected UTs but it may be more costly as the fund needs a guarantor, thus reducing the overall returns to the investors at the end of the period.

2.5.4 Front-end load fund vs Back-end load

Front-end load funds have the sales charge deducted immediately at the point of investing. Therefore an investment with a front-end load will get lesser units invested upfront. For example, if Amy wants to invest $10,000 of Fund A at 3% sales charge, the actual amount that will be used to purchase units will be $9,700 [Investment amount x (1- front end sales charge)].

Back-end load funds means the sales charge is made at the point of redemption or when the investor wants to exit. These are not common in Singapore. The investment amount and the immediate amount used to purchase units are the same. So the formula for net redemption proceeds will be [Redemption amount x (1- back end sales charge)].

Some back-end load funds offer lower sales charges if the investor holds for a longer period of time, and can even be zero if investor holds for over five years. For example, a fund may offer the following fees: if the investor holds for more than an entire year, the back end sales charge can be 4%, and if two years, the charges will be 3%, etc.

2.5.5 Single pricing vs Dual pricing

In the past, it was common to see many distributors display a single UT with two different prices. The lower price is called the "bid price" and the higher one is the "offer price." The difference is called the "bid-offer spread" and is usually 5%.

This caused some confusion among investors: what is the actual price of a unit of the fund? If an investor was thinking of buying, he or she would look at the offer price; if the investor was selling then he or she would use the bid price. I have heard some Singaporeans use the acronym "POSB" (purchase at offer, sell at bid) to remember this concept. Dual pricing is common for shares trading in Singapore.

Nowadays, for UT, a single price is more often displayed. This is the net asset value (NAV) of a unit. Let's assume a front-end load fund of 3% with no other charges. Peter wants to invest $10,000 into this fund, with a NAV of $1.623. He will receive approximately 5,976.58 units (the number of units he will be entitled = [Investment amount x (1- front end sales charge)]/NAV). The number of units is important for calculating 1) dividends if the fund is dividend-paying, and 2) the redemption amount when he wants to sell.

2.5.6 Daily priced and forward priced

Most UTs sold in Singapore are daily and forward priced. This means that the closing price of each day will be reflected the next business day. This happens because fund managers hold many securities within the fund and will need about one business day to update the accurate NAV of the fund and thus the corresponding NAV/unit.

When a UT transaction is performed before the cut-off time for the day (different times for different distributors and usually between 12 noon to 2 pm), the investor will transact at the closing price of that day, with the price only known at the end of the next business day. This is called forward pricing. The transacted price will be known on transacted date (t) plus one business day (T+1"). Therefore assuming the investor buys or sells the fund before cut-off on 5 March (Mon), he will only know the actual transacted price/unit one business day later. If 6 March (Tues) is a public holiday, then the investor will only get to know the confirmed price the following day, at the end of 7 March (Wed).

This is different from shares, which have price fluctuations within the day; the transacted price is based on real time changes and agreed prices and volume that the buyer and seller queue for. Therefore it is possible to buy the same company share at different prices on the same day. For UTs, this is impossible as there is only one price for each fund every trading day.

2.5.7 Currency Hedged vs Unhedged

UTs that invest in underlying securities traded in another currency (USD, EUR or JPY) may have another share class for Singaporean investors who like the UT objectives and holdings, but feel that the foreign currency may depreciate against the SGD. Thus they might opt for the SGD-Hedged or SGD-H share class option. This hedged class will have a slightly higher expense ratio or management fees for hedging costs, but investors will bear less currency risks fluctuations. There are less as opposed to totally zero currency risks as it is almost impossible to execute perfect currency swaps for any fund managers the whole year round.

Assume you have been optimistic on the value of Japanese equities since the beginning of 2013 when PM Abe implemented a series of economic reforms to stimulate the economy, one of which was to devalue the JPY to make their exports more competitive. So if you want the upside of Japanese equities without the weakening JPY (which happened for the next 6 to 12 months especially when the JPY weakened) to cancel or to reduce the gains when you convert to SGD (base currency), you should choose a Japanese equity UT that has a SGD-hedged class.

2.6 How to calculate the value of UTs

A newly-launched UT will plan to have a certain number of units issued, for example, 20 million units priced at $1. If demand is overwhelming and more than 20 million units are taken up, the fund managers will issue more units since most UTs sold in Singapore are open-ended. If response is lukewarm and fewer units are taken up, the fund manager will just issue fewer units and keep the launch price at $1 per unit.

The total raised funds will be the initial fund size or the assets under management by the fund manager. The fund manager will then proceed to invest these funds at the next dealing day according to the fund's investment objectives.

If the overall sum and value of the companies within the UT closed higher than the previous business day, then the NAV of the fund will appreciate since the number of issued units is still the same. The reverse is also true.

I mention overall sum because most UTs have over 40 different companies in their holdings, with each constituting a certain percentage weight of the fund's total AUM. This means that even if 2/3 of the companies within the fund drop in value, as long as the remaining 1/3 has a bigger percentage representation within the UT and their percentage gain is significant, the overall AUM and NAV of the fund may still rise.

2.7 Unit Trust Fees and Charges

Other than the bid-offer spread or the sales charge, there are other fees to take note of when investing in UT. Different distributors will have different fees; I list the more common ones and classify them in two main categories: a) Fees and charges paid by investors by reducing their units, and b) Fees and charges paid within the UT by reducing the unit NAV.

2.7.A1 Switching fee

Some distributors will impose a switching fee if the investor wants to switch out to buy another UT. The fee might be lower if it is switched to another UT within the same fund house versus a different fund house. Some distributors may charge a lower switching fee if it is switched to a lower risk UT versus switching to a higher risk UT.

The switching fee is similar to another round of sales charges. Even if the investor has lost, for example, 10% or more of his capital, or the switch is prompted by a representative of the distributor, the investor must still pay the switching fees.

2.7.A2 Wrap Account fees

Wrap accounts entitle the investor to unlimited free switching to all the funds within the distributors' platform. A dedicated financial adviser representative (FAR) is also assigned to help monitor and advice on the investor's portfolio. The wrap account fee per annum is a range of approximately 1% to 2% of the investor's total value of the UT portfolio.

The wrap fees, for example 1% per annum, is divided by trading days (approximately 250-2 depending on public holidays in that year = 0.004% per day, take 250 trading days). The distributor will aggregate the entire daily wrap fees to arrive at the total wrap fee for the investor's account for that quarter and charge it to the lowest risk fund (usually money market and bond funds in that order) within the investor's UT portfolio. If the investor's UT holdings are made up of UT from the same risk rating, then the quarterly wrap fee is deducted from the total units of the best performing UT in the portfolio.

The wrap account fees are usually pro-rated to the number of trading days. For example, if an investor decides to sell off and close the wrap account on the 123rd trading day of the year, he or she will only be charged for 123 days. This is different from the sales charge that is a one-time charge regardless of how long the investor has held the UT.

2.7.A3 Platform fees

Some investors undertake their own investments in an attempt to save on fees. However a platform fee (usually not on CPF investments, only on cash and Supplementary Retirement Scheme(SRS[4]) is hard to avoid and is approximately 0.3% to 0.5% p.a. of the investor's total value of the UT portfolio. The platform fee is paid to the distributor who provides the avenue and channel for investors to buy and sell UT, as well as offers a wide selection of funds from many different fund houses.

The platform fees are charged in the same way as the wrap fees above. Some distributors do not charge wrap and platform fees but they typically charge higher sales charge upfront and also switching fees.

2.7.A4 Central Providend Fund (CPF)-IA fees

If the investor invests with the CPF Ordinary Account or CPF Special Account excess funds,[5] he or she may get quarterly statements from his CPF Investment Agent (CPF-IA). The CPF-IA is the bank where the investor first opened his or her CPF investment account (DBS, OCBC or UOB).

As at the time of writing, CPF-IA charges investors using certain UT investment platforms like iFAST a flat fee of only SGD$2.14 every quarter, regardless of the number of funds and the amount invested. 100% of the CPF-IA fees go to the agent bank that helped the investor with the initial opening of the CPF Investment account. If the investment is made using cash/SRS, then are no CPF-IA fees.

Stricter rules that affected investor's use of CPF for UT purchases were passed in 2011. For the UT fund house to continue allowing investors to use their CPF OA and/or CPF SA funds or to keep their existing investors CPF monies as part of the fund size, they had to fulfill the following criteria: a) be the top 25% in performance and returns within their peer group (UTs with similar investment objectives and geographical investments), b) keep their expense ratio less than or equal to 1.95% for higher risk funds, 1.15% for low to medium funds and 0.65% for lower risk funds, c) have a sales charge of not more than 3%, and d) have a track record of at least three years.

This new ruling led to fewer fund choices for investors to invest for their CPF. However, for investors whom are less savvy or more particular about costs and expense ratio of UTs they invest in, they just need to look at UTs that are CPF investment approved to be assured that its past performance had been among the top quartile of its peer group and at least they will be paying lower sales charges and expense ratios.

2.7.B1 Management Fees

These are the fees charged by the fund manager and his or her team and usually range approximately 0.5% to 2% p.a. Bond UTs and UTs that track and replicate an index will have lower management fees. Most equity UT will have management fees of 1.5% per annum. The major component of management fees are the transaction and trading costs.

UT with a hedge fund strategy—where the fund manager uses complex financial structures or financial trading strategies (arbitrage, hedging, leverage, etc.) or uses several super computers each inputted with algorithms software to execute buy and sell trades—will typically have higher annual management fees closer to 2% per annum.

The annual management fee is calculated into the NAV of the fund on a daily basis (e.g., 1.5% divided by 250 trading days = 0.006% per day). So if the fund's NAV was supposed to be $2, the published daily NAV will be reflected as $1.99988 (1–0.006% x $2), without the investor having to pay additional cash or deducting their units.

2.7.B2 Trustee Fees

From the earlier chart on the structure of a UT, there is another party called the Trustee whose main role is to safeguard the assets of the funds and the interests of the investors. Trustees usually charge 0.1% to 0.15% per annum for their services. Trustee fees are calculated in the same way as management fees in B1), and are deducted from the daily published NAV of the UT.

2.7.B3 Performance Watermark Fees

An added incentive on top of the annual management fees for the fund managers to deliver results and grow the NAV of the fund. This fee is not common in Singapore and usually only charged by hedge fund UTs.

This is an example of performance fee of a real hedge fund UT factsheet: *"Up to 20% of the net new appreciation calculated and accrued on each valuation day but payable weekly."*

This means that the fund managers will be entitled to keep up to 20% of the new increase in the NAV of the unit, subject to the high watermark if today's close was higher than yesterday's close and so on. The fees are recorded but only deducted from the NAV after a week.

Mon	Tues	Wed	Thu	Fri
$1.78	$1.85	$1.76	$1.83	$1.89

In my opinion, the performance fee is a double-edged sword. On one hand it directly incentivises the fund manager and the team to deliver outstanding returns. However it compels them to take excessive risks; if a wrong call is made or they try to average down before they decide to cut loss and close the losing position totally, it may be too late. They may end up chalking big losses that will reduce their NAV per unit, which may take years to recover. One way to make performance fees benefit investors invested in hedge fund UTs is to ensure the fees are paid only if the fund has recovered all its previous losses and is back to its inception price or the price that it closed at the end of its very first day or performance fee will be paid out only if the UT returns 6% that year and it will be a fraction of the profits above 6%.

In this example, Tuesday's closing price is higher than Monday's, hence the performance fee owing to the fund managers is 20% of ($1.85 − $1.78) = $0.014 per unit. Assuming there are 20 million issued units, they would have earned $0.014 x 20 million = $28,000 extra as performance fee on a single day. On Wednesday, there is no performance fee because the price dropped. There will be performance fees charged for Thursday and Friday. The performance fees accrue for the week whenever today's closing price is higher than yesterday's closing price.

2.7.B4 Annual Expense Ratio (AER)

Since there are many fees and charges in a UT and it may be tedious to calculate them individually, how can investors know the expenses of the UT? Thankfully there is the Annual Expense Ratio (AER) to help investors make an informed decision so they can be more mindful of selecting UTs with lower costs. All else being constant, a fund with a lower AER will give better returns than a fund with higher AER in the long run. The AER only shows fees that are paid within the UT by NAV reduction.

The AER is the annual total expenses of the UT divided by the UT's total assets averaged out for the year. The total expenses include the fund manager's fees, custodian fees, transaction fees of buying and selling the companies inside the UT holdings, auditing fees, legal fees, etc. The AER can change yearly since the denominator is the UT's total average assets; if the UT experiences a big influx of new investor funds due to analyst recommendations, then the AER would certainly drop further and the UT will be seen as a more 'efficient' investment.

Almost all UTs in Singapore publish their AER as long as the UT exists for over a year. This can be found in the fund details section in the online platform of most distributors, or you can enquire from the fund house. The average AERs are as follows: for a low risk money market, about 0.32%; SGD bond fund, about 0.63%; a high yield bond fund, about 1.53%; an equity fund, about 1.75%. The hedge fund with the performance watermark discussed in the earlier section has an AER of 4.01%. A direct correlation usually exist, the higher the risk rating of the UT, the higher will also be its AER as more transactions are performed by the fund managers.

Assume an investor receives a tip from a friend and is interested in investing in Asia Pacific, excluding Japan equities, and in particular the small and medium companies sector. He will run through an online filter and get a few UTs that fit his criteria. Upon careful study, he may be surprised that United Asian Growth Opportunities fund has an AER of 1.43% while DWS Asian Small/Mid Cap UT has an AER of 2.17%, more than 1.5 times higher! The other UT that will appear is Aberdeen Asian Smaller Companies, with AER of 1.83%. From this example, we can tell that different fund houses have different AER although they may share similar investment objectives, the same investment geographical boundaries and investing in the same small and medium companies sector of the economy.

Key learning points

- It is important to always look at the name of the UT fund and its investment objectives.
- Note the roles of the parties in a UT structure
- Be familiar with commonly used terms in UT
- Always be aware of common fees and the charges of a UT. Take note of a UT's Annual Expense Ratio (AER), and remember that a lower AER means lower expenses and more superior returns in the long run.

Endnotes

4. Supplementary Retirement Scheme (SRS) is a voluntary contribution scheme to complement the CPF. It was started in 2001.
5. As at the time of writing, only amounts in excess of $20,000 in CPF Ordinary Account and $40,000 in CPF Special Account can be used for investments. The CPF is a compulsory comprehensive savings plan for working Singaporeans and permanent residents to fund their retirement, healthcare and housing needs.

Why Buy Unit Trusts

3.1 Lack of time and knowledge

As all investment decisions (what, when, at what price and how much to buy and sell) are all made by a professional unit trust (UT) fund manager with analysts' inputs; all the investor needs to do is to select a UT with an investment objective that he or she understands and is confident will appreciate in the near future. Many working adults cite this as one of the top reasons for investing in UTs.

Furthermore, to counter a lack of time and knowledge, some investors chose to buy UT via a representative. He/she will have fewer choices to make as the licensed professional representative would have shortlisted, filtered out and made recommendations on suitable UTs after a round of fact-finding to better understand the investor's objectives, risk appetite, investment time horizon and current portfolio, etc.

To overcome a lack of knowledge, investors can read investment books, download free research articles, and attend free educational seminars and talks from online UT platforms. Investors will be poised to make a more informed decisions if they have greater knowledge of current affairs and economic news, as well as an understanding of a UT's investment philosophy, top holdings and geographical regions.

3.2 Unfamiliar markets

Investors unfamiliar with the investment climate (companies, local economy or regulations) of some geographical regions of the world will benefit greatly by having the local knowledge and expertise of the UT fund manager.

For example, a Singaporean investor who is optimistic on Brazilian equities and believes they will do well in the next 12 months can either buy a passive Brazil exchange traded fund (ETF) that tracks the Brazil Bovespa or an actively managed UT that invests in single country Brazil equities. Compared to investors based in Singapore who may not even have visited Brazil before, a local UT fund manager and his/her team of analysts who has grew up or lived in that region will definitely be more knowledgeable and familiar with the investment climate and can react faster to the news and rebalance their investment portfolio .

3.3 Bad experience with stocks or other investment assets

Some investors who got burnt investing in other asset classes (e.g., stocks or FX) become lifelong anti-investments advocates in that asset class and flock over to UTs.

One common reason many investors get burnt is acting on 'hot tips' from colleagues, friends or brokers without finding out whether the investment is actually suitable for them. Their mind is blinded by the amazing returns that friends and colleagues claim to have received. Greed for a slice of the pie takes over rational thinking and analysis, causing them to overlook the risks and other negative aspects of the investment. This herd mentality is dangerous and often results in overspeculation (see the Blumont example in section 1.3).

It is like the analogy of learning to ride a bicycle, if your child falls the first few times, will you tell your child to give up and not learn to ride a bicycle forever? There is a Chinese saying translated as where you fall down, where you should pick yourself up again. Learn and understand the reason for the fall: is it attributed to the terrain (investment climate at that time), the bicycle (type of investment) or even human factors like the rider overestimating his/her skills (investor overestimating his risk tolerance and knowledge)?

Investors need to understand that different asset classes perform differently at different times. So even if they lost money in shares or structured products, it does not mean they will lose money in UT. They should also not be complacent if they made money as their investments might still underperform the index and benchmark. A famous investment adage goes: 'A rising tide lifts all boats'; thus one should never confuse brilliance in a bull market, as anyone can make money in such upbeat markets.

3.4 Diversification

Many investors prefer UT over stocks for its diversification benefits for the same amount of capital invested. A typical regional equity UT can have exposure to equities in more than eight countries. Country diversification is important as there may be country specific risks like political crisis, interest rate risk, currency risk, economic risks due to natural disaster, etc. Hence by investing in a UT with exposure to several countries, specific country risks are greatly reduced.

Regional- and country-specific UTs also enjoy sector diversification benefits: they can have exposure to over six different sectors of the economy. The usual heavyweight sectors in most UTs are Financials, Consumer discretionary, IT, Healthcare, etc. When the investor invests in a UT, he/she trusts the fund manager to be up-to-date on the news affecting the sectors of the economy in the country and act to grow the value of the UT and consequently the UT's NAV per unit. The benefits of good sector diversification are important as different sectors of the economy perform better during different market phases.

3.5 Low barriers to entry and low costs for economies of scale investing

Other than hedge fund UTs, UTs have probably one of the lowest barriers of entry wealth instruments in Singapore. Although share lot sizes have been recently reduced to 100 to encourage greater participation in the stock market, it will be dufficult to replicate a portfolio of 30 to 40 securities like a UT fund as it will incur high transaction costs (the investor has to pay for 30 to 40 trades of 100 shares at the current minimum of $25+ GST per trade).

The investor might be better off incurring the one-time upfront sales charge of a UT and enjoy economies of scale in the investment. Furthermore, the stock market entails not only transaction costs, but also headache, hassle and time taken to manually queue 30 securities, including adjusting the price and volume as intraday prices of securities might change dramatically; the investor may also have to input his queue and trade for a single security for a few days before he buys the security at the price and volume he wants. Ask any investor who has bought Singapore shares online before how challenging it is to monitor and buy just five securities in a week during trading hours! Moreover, stress, plus distraction at work, might result in a disastrous mistake like inputting one more zero in the volume or keying in the wrong price to queue for shares. I have never heard such horror stories from investors buying UTs.

Some UTs require the minimum of $1 000 investment to start, even then investors can easily sidestep this requirement by signing up for a regular savings plan (RSP). RSP can accumulate the investor's wealth and only require a min of $100/UT/month to get started. Anyone over the age of 18 can open a single name account to start investing in UT in Singapore to enjoy economies of scale in transaction costs because of the fund manager's trading frequency and bulk transactions.

For investors who like the idea of regular investing, but prefer stocks over UTs, POEMs as of this time of writing has a monthly RSP scheme called "Share Builder plus". It gives investors a choice to invest up to 20 counters monthly, these counters are the big industry leaders that also makes up Singapore Straits Times Index. (STI) More information is available at http://www.poems.com.sg/rsp/Share-Builders-Plan.html, do check the fees and charges tab too. Investors opting for Share Builder plus must note that the fixed counters lack flexibility and they will still have to monitor market events for opportunities and threats.

3.6 Clear and independent structure

UTs that are marketed for sale in Singapore are established by a trust deed, which sets out the roles and parties in the UT structure. With the trustee and auditors independent of the fund managers keeping close tabs on where, what, why and how the fund manager manages the monies and complies within the fund mandate and investment objectives, investors can sleep better knowing that checks and controls are in place.

The setup of the roles and parties in the UT structure gives it an edge over individual company securities. Consider the regularity with which the public hears about frauds, rigging, accounting scandals, etc. taking place, even in big listed organisations. It is less likely with UTs. Even if one of the security within the UT is investigated for suspected fraud or mismanagements, and comprise a substantial percentage (assuming 8% which is already very rare, unless it is an emerging market single country UT) of the UT's total AUM, the UT's NAV may just drop slightly as they still have 92% of the UT's AUM in other securities. The only exception is an industry-wide or sector-wide fraud. In such a case the UT's NAV obviously will take more of a beating.

Selling UTs in Singapore is a regulated activity by the Monetary Authority of Singapore (MAS) as representatives of Financial Advisors have to pass exams and be of good financial standing and good moral integrity. Sellers of other types of investments, like land banking, wine investments and other forms of multi-level marketing products are much less regulated.

3.7 Specialized investments

Some hedge fund UTs managed by fund managers who are experts in certain investment strategies like arbitrage techniques (simultaneous buy and sell an identical or similar asset to exploit a pricing difference in different markets due to markets not operating at 100% efficiency all the time) or spotting the Mergers and Acquisition (M&A) space to buy companies before they become targets of takeover, thereby delivering profits for the investors. These managers rely on proprietary computer systems and pre-set algorithms that prompt them to take action when certain prices are triggered or certain corporate actions or market events happen. This is almost impossible to replicate or for the untrained investors to do it themselves, thus the way to profit is to jump on the bandwagon and invest collectively in these hedge fund UTs.

3.8 Currency-hedged class options available

Some UTs offers several different currency share classes[6] for the same fund. Most of the share class usually comes with a Singapore dollar currency hedged feature and are denominated with SGD-Hedged or SGD-H as an extension to their fund name (*see* section 2.5.7). UTs with a currency-hedged class are good for investors who want to invest in the country's equities but are not optimistic on the outlook of its currency against the SGD. In other words, they do not want currency fluctuations to affect their gains or losses.

For Singapore investors who are confident of the UT's performance and also feel that UT's denominated foreign currency[7] will strengthen against their base SGD currency, UTs gives them the option to invest in a non-SGD hedged class to further enhance their gains from the currency appreciation if they are correct. For example, a Singaporean investor is optimistic on US equities and USD against SGD because by early 2014, it has become public knowledge that the US FED will stick to their plan to reduce monthly bond purchases and eventually raise interest rates, which will cause the USD to appreciate, thus the investor should invest in Fidelity America SGD UT instead of Fidelity America SGD Hedged class UT.

3.9 Possible to use CPF OA/SA and SRS

Investing in UT is popular in Singapore because of the option to use our CPF OA (Ordinary Account), CPF SA (Special Account) and SRS (Supplementary Retirement Scheme) to make investments (*see* chapter 2, note 5). Balances above $20,000 in the CPF OA and $40,000 in the CPF SA can be invested.

I urge investors to be careful in the use of CPF SA to invest as the current interest the CPF Board pays is 4% per annum for

CPF SA balances and 2.5% for CPF OA. Therefore if the investor uses the CPF SA, he/she is giving up a risk-free guaranteed rate of 4% to invest in an instrument that may not give the same amount of returns after charges or worse still may have negative returns.

I would urge all Singaporeans, Permanent Residents and also foreigners with a taxable income of $60,000 or more per annum to open a SRS account.[8] Based on the Singapore income tax rates for 2014, anyone with a taxable income of $60,000 in the previous year needs to pay approximately $1,950 in taxes. If he/she contributes to the SRS the annual maximum allowable contribution for Singaporeans/PRs of $12,750, then his/her tax for that year will only be approximately $1,057.5, a savings of $892.50. For a foreigner who can contribute up to $29,750, and assuming he/she does that, then for the same $60,000 taxable income, he/she only needs to pay $208.75 in taxes, significantly lower than $1,950! All these calculations are made without including the personal tax rebate of up to $1,500 or 30% rebate for taxpayers below age of 60 and 50% for taxpayers above 60 (whichever rebate is lower) because we do not know when and if the Singapore Government and Ministry of Finance will stop extending this rebate.

Higher income earners with taxable income >$160,000 a year will benefit more with SRS contributions. At $160,000, they will be paying approximately $13,950 in taxes. Assuming they make the current maximum SRS contribution of $12,750, their tax payable will drop to $12,037.50: a fantastic savings of $1,912.5. This equates to a 15% impressive tax savings on $12,750, very attractive considering there are no investments giving guaranteed returns of even 6% p.a. now.

The Ministry of Finance recently announced in Budget 2015 that they will raise the current ceiling for voluntary SRS contributions for Singaporeans and PRs to $15,300 and $35,700 respectively. This is good news for investors already contributing the maximum of $12,750 every year; they will get to enjoy more tax savings if they contribute more with the revised ceiling from 1 Jan 2016.

Other than the obvious tax savings from SRS contributions, monies in the SRS can also be used to invest in UTs, shares,

ETFs, REITs, insurance, etc. If the monies were left untouched, the returns will only be the prevailing rate of ordinary savings account of the SRS operator, which has been 0.1% to 0.2% per annum for a long time and will never beat inflation.

The latest 2001 to 2013 SRS statistics from the Ministry of Finance (*see* table below) and composition of SRS portfolios is encouraging: total SRS contributions have been increasing steadily over the last 13 years from S$160 million in Dec 2001 to S$4,340 million in Dec 2013. This is a growth of 27 times, even though the number of account holders has only grown 7.7 times from 11,890 to 91,652. This is probably due to most SRS holders continuing to contribute the full amount every year after they have made their initial contribution. This trend seems set to continue.

However there is also a 'disturbing' sign: over the years the balance at year end in the form of cash has been more than 30% of total SRS contributions except for 2005 to 2009. Hopefully it is due to many SRS account holders rushing to contribute in December before the year-end cut-off who are just waiting for the right time and opportunity to invest, and not because they intend to hold their SRS as cash balance for the long run.

Another trend is that UT and insurance as a percentage of total SRS composition used to be higher from 2002 to 2009, but SRS account holders seems to favour shares, REITs and ETFs over UT and insurance from 2009 to 2013. This could be due to a low global interest rates environment, booming property prices in the last four years before Singapore government's cooling measures on the property sector and also REITs mandated distribution of at least 90% of taxable income.[9] Although the proportion of SRS investment in UT dropped to 9% in Dec 2013, in absolute amounts invested, there is still a rise over the years from $17.6 million in Dec 2001 to $390.6 million by Dec 2013.

	Cumulative SRS Statistics as at:												
	Dec-01	Dec-02	Dec-03	Dec-04	Dec-05	Dec-06	Dec-07	Dec-08	Dec-09	Dec-10	Dec-11	Dec-12	Dec-13
No of A/c holders	11,890	16,548	24,383	27,770	31,413	35,762	41,334	46,442	53,656	63,984	71,865	82,512	91,652
Total SRS Contributions (billion S$)	0.16	0.31	0.55	0.74	0.95	1.17	1.44	1.72	2.05	2.49	3.01	3.64	4.34
Composition of SRS investment portfolio (at cost) (%)													
Cash	59%	33%	34%	34%	24%	22%	22%	25%	28%	30%	32%	35%	34%
UT (%)/ Absolute UT invested (billion S$)	11%/ 0.0176	16%/ 0.0496	16%/ 0.088	16%/ 0.1184	19%/ 0.1805	18%/ 0.2106	16%/ 0.2304	14%/ 0.2408	12%/ 0.246	11%/ 0.2739	9%/ 0.2709	9%/ 0.3276	9%/ 0.3906
Insurance	28%	44%	40%	40%	39%	37%	34%	32%	30%	28%	26%	25%	23%
Fixed Deposit	1%	3%	2%	2%	6%	7%	6%	5%	4%	3%	2%	2%	1%
Shares, REITs, ETFs	1%	4%	8%	8%	9%	10%	12%	14%	16%	19%	22%	21%	24%
Others	0	0	1%	1%	3%	6%	9%	10%	10%	10%	9%	8%	8%
Age profile of SRS holders (%)													
21–35	14%	14%	14%	13%	12%	12%	12%	12%	11%	11%	11%	10%	11%
36–45	41%	38%	38%	37%	36%	35%	35%	34%	34%	33%	33%	32%	31%
46–55	38%	38%	37%	37%	36%	36%	35%	35%	36%	35%	35%	35%	34%
56–61	7%	9%	10%	12%	14%	14%	15%	15%	14%	14%	15%	15%	15%
≥ 62	0	1%	1%	1%	2%	2%	3%	4%	5%	6%	7%	8%	8%
Nationality of SRS holders (%)													
Foreigners	1%	2%	2%	2%	2%	2%	2%	3%	3%	3%	3%	3%	4%
Singapore PRs	11%	11%	11%	12%	12%	12%	12%	12%	12%	12%	12%	12%	12%
Singaporeans	87%	87%	87%	86%	86%	86%	86%	85%	85%	85%	85%	85%	84%

Source: app.mof.gov.sg/data/cmsresource/Our%20Policy/SRS/
Cumulative%20SRS%20Statistics%202013.pdf

3.10 Longevity and popularity for dividends as passive income

As discussed earlier, more SRS account holders are investing their SRS monies into REITs since end 2009 and it seems to be an ongoing trend. The first REIT in Singapore was started only in July 2002. End December 2013, there were a total of 29 listed REITs on the Singapore Stock Exchange, of which 18 of them had IPO dates after 1 Jan 2010. This reflects the popularity of this sector among Singapore investors with more IPOs in the last four years.

Let's use the Philip Singapore Real Estate Income fund as an example. Started in Sept 2011, this UT has a fund size of approximately S$44.21 million as of 8 Aug 2014 and holds a portfolio of over ten Singapore industrial, office and retail REITs. The quarterly dividends that this UT has been paying out is between 15 to 15.8 cents per unit, which is about 4.87% per annum assuming no sales charge and the purchase price of $1.2952/unit. For $100,000 invested, the dividend payout will be approx $4,870 a year, a pretty decent stream of passive retirement income for most Singaporeans as we are also living longer.

Although the dividend rate of 4.87% for Philip Singapore Real Estate Income UT is slightly lower than the average dividend payout of 6.02% among the 26 REITs in the last quarterly payout in July 2014, the advantage of the UT over a single counter REIT is the diversification across different class of Singapore Real Estate. As of May 2014, its portfolio consists of 26.88% retail, 23.15% office, 25.6% industrials and 7.13% hotels, the rest are mixed developments and cash, therefore greatly reducing the risk of a particular sector of real estate not doing well and also potential single company key executive or management risk.

3.11 Opportunity cost of inaction

Singapore's average interest rate from 1938 to 2014 was 1.68%, hardly able to be on par with inflation rate of approximately 2.8% from 1962 to 2014. From the chart below, we can see that Singapore's interest rate in the last 10 years from Jan 2005 is even lower, and has not been able to cross 5%. I would think the post-global financial crisis in 2008 marked the start of an era of low interest rates for developed nations. In fact, there is a double whammy situation: we have both lower and lower interest rates, if we compare the decades from the 80s to the 90s to 2000s, and rising inflation rates, although the reported inflation rate by Statistics Singapore is 2.8% from 1962 to 2014. Ask any lower- and middle-income household in Singapore and many will say that inflation felt more like 3% to 4% per annum.

Although Singapore's interest rates will likely rise eventually from 2015 or 2016, taking a cue from current US Fed Chief Ms Janet Yellen's intention to raise US interest rates after seeing US economy reach certain milestones, it is unlikely we will be able to see SGD Fixed Deposit rates returning to more than 4% per annum any time soon. Warren Buffett once said, "The one thing I will tell you is the worst investment you can have is cash... Cash is going to be worth less over time". People who hold cash equivalents today may feel safe, but they have opted for a terrible long-term asset that pays virtually nothing and is certain to depreciate in value.

Thus if Singapore investors remain passive and keep their monies in savings accounts and fixed deposits, in the long term they are unlikely to beat real inflation rate, which is typically higher than many ASEAN neighbours. We know Singapore is a small nation vulnerable to cost-push inflation as we import most of our food, raw materials, oil and energy, etc. Persistently high rates of inflation year on year will lead to companies adjusting the selling price of their goods and services very often, which in turn leads to employees demanding pay raises etc. So to keep up with their real standard of living, some employees in jobs with low bargaining power will be worst hit and can cause social problems and strife.

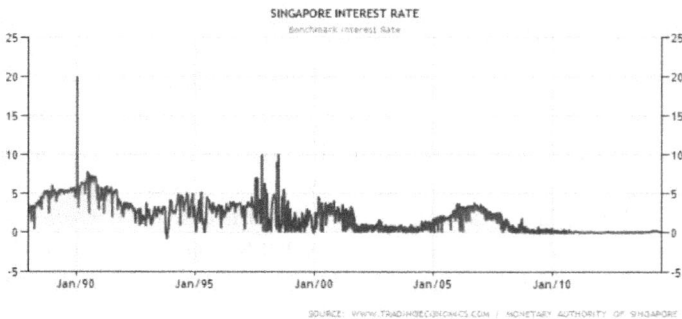

SINGAPORE INTEREST RATE
Benchmark interest Rate

SOURCE: WWW.TRADINGECONOMICS.COM / MONETARY AUTHORITY OF SINGAPORE

From 2006, the rapid increase in Singapore's population also led to raised demand and inflationary pressures on basic goods like public housing and utilities, and an increased strain on the transport infrastructure leading to higher COEs for all form of vehicles and public transport fee hikes. Thus depositors who have their monies in savings accounts in the banks experienced a decline in their real purchasing power of goods and services.

The Fidelity Global Inflation-linked bond UT is popular with investors whom are concerned to have their investments keep pace with global inflation. The objective of this UT is to generate an attractive real level of income and capital appreciation by utilising a range of strategies from within, amongst others, the global inflation linked, interest rates and credit markets. The UT was started in July 2008 and has delivered approximately 2.7% per annum, not factoring sales charge. The top 10 holdings are US Treasury notes and more than 93.71% are rated AA and AAA.

Key learning points

The common reasons why people buy UT are:

- Personal (lack of time and expertise, unfamiliar markets or bad experience with other asset class

- Benefits of UT (diversification, low amounts to start investing, clear and independent structure of UT, specialised investments in hedge funds and availability of currency hedge class)

- Other factors (availability to use CPF and SRS to buy UT, longevity and popularity of regular dividends for passive income and opportunity cost of inaction)

- There may be more than these 11 reasons for people to buy UT, so if you agree with a few of them, you can start researching or get in touch with a good representative. If you already have UTs, you can consider reviewing your portfolio and revisit your reasons for buying them in the past and take appropriate action now.

Endnotes

6. For convenience, investors who already have money in a particular currency, and do not wish to convert it for the sake of investing in that UT, can buy the fund using different currencies. For example the Allianz Income and Growth fund allows investors to use SGD, AUD, RMB and USD to invest.
7. Investors can invest in Fidelity America fund with USD, SGD-Hedged or SGD. As all their holdings are US firms in US dollars, so investors who are bullish/optimistic on US Equities doing better and that the USD will strengthen more than SGD should buy Fidelity USD Fund (SGD class) to get higher returns vs Fidelity USD Fund (SGD-Hedged) class.
8. Please refer to app.mof.gov.sg/supplementary_retirement_scheme.aspx for more information on SRS terms and conditions and to download the booklets and flyers for a more comprehensive explanation.
9. It is mandatory for all Singapore listed REITs to give at least 90% of their taxable income every year out as dividends to shareholders.

Five Common Mistakes and Five Winning Tips

4.1 Five Common Investment Mistakes

As the saying goes, "we should learn from the mistakes of others, we won't live long enough to make them all ourselves." There are more than five factors that may cause a UT investment to be a mistake, I have listed them here so we can avoid stepping into the pit that others before us have fallen into; this will save us considerable money and heartache.

4.1.1 Unclear on the investment objectives before purchase

The key to a good start and a happy investment experience is for investors to understand their investment goals (is this investment for retirement, or your childrens' education, or for the downpayment of a car, etc.), its required time frame, and their risk tolerance.[10]

Investors should also understand a UT's investment objectives and risks, and ensure that they are in line with his/her personal investment objectives. They should also be aware of the UT's fees and charges. The investor should also read up on the fund manager's background and track record, especially his/her funds' performance during different market cycles compared to other peer UTs. Does the fund manager possess enough expertise and experience to manage the UT according to its objectives? Although past performance is not indicative of future performance, it does not hurt to see the consistency of the fund manager's track record during his/her tenure managing the UT. If the UT has a track record of over ten years, look at how it performed during periods of crisis (the post Sept 2001 terror attack, the SARs period in Mar 2003, the 2008 global financial meltdown and the latest 2012 Eurozone Austerity crisis).

Other than studying the fund manager's background and the UT's record, it's important to also look at the fund house, as it is the organisation the fund manager and analysts are working for. More established fund houses have an impressive track record of generating decades upon decades of stellar performances from the systems and human experience they have built up during numerous market cycles. It's good that the investors do their due diligence and check these points before they purchase the UT.

4.1.2 Over-trusting a Financial Adviser Representative (FAR)

If the investor is dealing with a representative from a bank, insurance firm or a financial advisory firm, always ask for his/ her name card and representative number. The name card should state the financial adviser's firm that he/she is representing. Go to the Monetary Authority of Singapore (MAS) website[11] and check if the firm is licensed and regulated by MAS, and which services they are authorised to conduct. You can also review the firm's website, beliefs, merits, any negative news and publicity as well as the background of key appointment holders.

After the investor is comfortable with the company information, verify the background and qualifications of the FAR. Every representative has a MAS Rep No. and investors can check if the representative is indeed appointed by the said financial adviser firm,[12] how long he/she has been with the company and the regulated activities that the representative is authorised to perform. The status of the representative should be "appointed"; any other status should cause alarm, so do check the legend below the webpage for its definition. He/she can also call the financial adviser firm the next day to verify the status of the representative.

The investor can also click on the MAS enforcement action tab to see if there were any MAS enforcement actions taken against the individual. If there are records, the investor should read the record before deciding whether to do business with the FAR. Investors should always do their due diligence and read up more or asked to be shown proof of actual returns or quantifiable evidence as claimed by the FAR.

4.1.3 Herd mentality investing

Remember the old Wall Street investment adage: "No trees grow to the sky". Another reason investments sour is because some investors follow published information and chase after past top performers in the form of single country or single sector UTs that have performed very well in the past. No matter its past performance, no investment offers a guarantee of replicating its performance infinitely. Since economies are cyclical in nature and go through phases, any sector/country that had already performed well in the last few quarters and years may be on the verge of becoming a laggard. Conversely, a laggard sector or country UT may be on the verge of a turnaround after restructuring its economy or management, or after certain political changes or technology advances.

When investors buy stocks, many like to look at the Price/Earnings per share ratio (P/E) for the price other investors in the market are willing to pay for the company's share for each dollar of earnings. A high P/E ratio indicates the stock is overpriced assuming ceteris paribus. It must be noted at this point to compare P/E ratio of companies within the same industry as each industry represents different growth prospects (e.g., financial companies should not be compared against utilities companies). Usually equities that were the flavors of the year or top returns last year will have very high P/E ratio, inviting questions as to whether the company can generate earnings growth in line with its share price growth.

Likewise, for equity UTs, because it is made up of a portfolio of companies often in different sectors in their holdings, P/

E ratios cannot be used in the same way. Instead I suggest investors *look at the current NAV of the UT they have shortlisted and compare against the 1 year, 3 years and all-time high and low NAV* to get a good indication whether the UT's current NAV is overpriced.[13] The investor should be forward looking and ask at which stage is the global economy now and where are the next growth countries/regions or sectors to invest in them instead of past flavours of the year.

For example, an investor is optimistic on single country Korean equities growth, believing that as USA economy recovers it will likely demand more electronics and cars (Samsung and Hyundai). Perhaps the investor only wishes to invest in SGD currency. He/she can use the search/filter tool to sift out UTs invested predominantly in Korean equities: (Franklin Templeton Korea fund, HGIF Korean Equity and LionGlobal Korea fund), so just like comparing P/E ratios within industry, investors should compare 1-year, 3-year and all-time high NAV vs current NAV within similar UTs.

Timing the market is another classic form of herd mentality investing. Many people think that by studying charts and trends or by following the investments of their friends or colleagues who attended technical analysis courses, they will be able to successfully time and beat the market. In reality, no one has either successfully timed the market ten out of ten times or predicted when exactly markets will peak and trough. Not even the legendary investor Mr Buffett, who famously said, "People that think they can predict the short-term movement of the stock market, or listen to other people who talk about timing the market, they are making a big mistake."

Therefore what is more achievable than timing the market is diversification across different asset classes, geography and sectors; investing in regular intervals; and regular portfolio review with rebalancing.

4.1.4 Excessive conservatism vs excessive risk taking

Neither of these two opposing approaches toward investing will make an investor very successful over time. Excessive conservatism is displayed by people who never want to invest and save all their money in the bank; but with current low interest rates banks offer for deposits, coupled with high inflation rates, the saver will find it hard to attain real growth of wealth in 20–30 years.

Excessive risk taking should also be discouraged, even if it is on a hot tip recommended by friends or the broker. When given a hot tip, an investor should remember the first rule of investing: *only invest with monies that he/she can afford to lose*. If it is a volatile investment above the usual risk tolerance the investor can accept, and it keeps him/her up at night, it is considered as an excessive risk. Using leverage to achieve greater gains but with risks above one's level of comfort is another form of excessive risk taking that must be avoided. Even Buffett famously said he would not sacrifice his sleep for the chance of extra profits through leverage.

Instead of becoming overly fearful or overly greedy, the investor must develop both financial reasoning (the science of investing), as well as be guided by intuition, risk-taking and inventiveness (the art of investing). Analyse the top 10 holdings of the UT individually, find out more about the geographical allocation of the UT, and ask yourself if you see future growth in that economy. If the investment currency of the UT is not in SGD, analyse other currencies too. For example, one could study USD/SGD or EUR/SGD historical charts for exchange rates or read some currency's analyst outlook. Use the analyst reports as a reference and importantly, consider if it is sensible and accurate. Do research on the fund managers and also their past track record managing the UT, etc.

4.1.5 Not monitoring your investments

Some investors neglect to review their portfolio and perform at least one annual rebalancing; if markets are turbulent, the review and rebalance should be done more frequently. Although buy and hold strategy still has its place in the twenty-first century, a portion of the investor's monies can be placed in an actively managed and constantly rebalanced account, overseen by a FAR. This account can contain the more volatile regional equities, single country and single sector UTs that requires closer and constant monitoring.

Many analysts and experts have said that market cycles have become increasingly shorter with more wild swings. This is due to technological advances and super computers executing hundreds of trade in a second, which was unheard of prior to the nineties. Information is now everywhere, and fund managers and big investors react to financial news in an instant. Not monitoring your investments regularly is costly and you do not want to be left holding that UT after 50% or more of the investors have sold their investments and the music had stopped.

4.2 Five tips to build your dream portfolio and get consistent positive returns

After discussing a couple of investment mistakes to avoid, let's discuss some behaviours that we can adopt to build our very own dream portfolios. As everyone of us is unique, with different investment objectives and goals, time frames as well as risk tolerance, etc., there is no perfect portfolio that appeals to everyone. Taking a couple of ideas from this section and implement and customising them along the way is much better than reading, knowing and not doing a single thing after. Remember, everyone who works hard for their money deserves to have that dream portfolio working hard for them too.

4.2.1 Choose a manager with similar investment style and beliefs

After the investor is crystal clear on his/her unique objectives, the next question to ask is if the investor is comfortable with the investment style of the fund manager. This is to shortlist that few funds for a closer examination from the >400 UTs available to investors in Singapore. There is not much proof to conclude that certain fund manager's investment styles are better than others.

The more common investment styles of fund managers are:

4.2.1.1 Large vs small capitalisation

This refers to their expertise in selecting equities in that country or region, whether the fund they are managing only buys into large cap or small cap firms. Companies with over $10 billion in market value are currently referred to as "large cap". The exact definition and size of large cap may differ slightly among the different fund houses, especially when market value changes daily because of the changes in share price. More often than not, the fund factsheet and product highlight sheet will state the size range for small cap or medium cap that the fund managers can invest in.

4.2.1.2 Global vs regional vs single country

This refers to the geographical area of equities or bonds that the fund manager has expertise in and can invest their investor's monies.

4.2.1.3 Top-down vs bottom-up

This is the investment approach and preference of different managers to derive the shortlist of stocks to consider for investments. Some will select stocks from a Top-down approach, which usually means they will start from looking at global and regional news and trends, especially what will affect certain sectors of the economy, and then analyse the impact of these on the geography of their investments. They then decide to rebalance their portfolio, whether to buy more stocks in the sector if it is positive outlook or to trim stocks if it is negative. Before they buy into the company's stock, they will also analyse the company's data and key statements.

Other managers adopt a Bottom-up approach to selecting stocks, the reverse of the Top-down approach. They will analyse the company's key ratios and statements (P/E ratio, P/L Statement, Balance sheets, Cash Flow Statements, etc.) and if these are attractive, they may even meet-up with the key appointment holders of the company (CEO, COO and CFO, etc.) and do a site visit of the company to better understand its operations and vision. They will then look at the news, trends and global views to see if it supports the appreciation of the stock price in the near to medium term, or conversely may be detrimental to the stock price. The fund manager then decides to invest in the stock or to move on and select other stocks in the shortlist.

4.2.1.4 Capital appreciation vs income orientec

This refers to the fund manager's experience and preference to pick stocks based on price appreciation of the stock or on the income based on the dividends of the stock.

4.2.1.5 Value vs growth

Fund managers with a value investing style will select stocks when they feel that their current prices are lower than its reasonable price. They are on the lookout for bargains and overlooked opportunities. Warren Buffett, arguably the most well known and most successful investor to date is an advocate of value investing and comes from the same camp and school of thought as his mentor: Benjamin Graham. Most investors and managers that subscribe to value investing tend to favour stocks with an easy to understand business model, a stable business operations, and a good track record.

Managers and investors from the growth investing camp, however, they tend to favour companies with higher P/E ratios or companies that will seem to thrive on long-term trends and changes in technology, social demographics, government regulations, etc. The benefits of a growth strategy is better potential and appreciation if the right call is made and market sentiments echo the growth managers views too. However, managers that adopt the growth strategy tend to select stocks that are already trading at a premium, and in fact they are likely higher than their fair or book value. These companies' stocks are also usually more volatile; if earnings do not meet expectations, their price may suffer a significant setback as compared to stocks that are selected by a value manager.

With different selection, management styles and beliefs among the fund managers of different func house, the investor have to ask himself which approach resonates and is the best 'fit' for him/her. In my opinion, the fundamentals must be well aligned to have a good start and investor experience before the profits even come in.

4.2.2 Track and be watchful of fees and charges vs potential benefits

A difference of just 1% p.a. compounded over 35 years can result in vastly different outcome for the retirement nest egg of John and Jim. (Assume both of them are disciplined savers and have been saving $500/month in the same UT funds for the last 35 years, John is able to get an annualised average return of 5%, Jim's net returns is 4% as he incur higher fees and charges that John paid lesser.) At the end of the investment period, John would have ended up with $541,921.84 vs Jim $441,913.35—a staggering difference of $100k. Although both get back more than their invested capital of $210,000, all of us would prefer to be in John's shoes. Remember our earlier discussion on UT fees, charges and AER: the investor should thus always choose a UT with lower fees and charges to maximise his/her returns.

Another ratio to be mindful of when looking at costs of a UT is *turnover ratio,* especially important for equity and alternative UTs. The turnover ratio is the percentage of the portfolio that is bought and sold yearly, and is found in most UT's prospectus. Although the AER of UTs already account for transaction costs (of which turnover ratio is a major contributor of total transaction costs), it may be alarming if the UT turnover ratio is >50%. This indicates high transaction costs; imagine over half of the holdings being entirely different year on year! Would the UT fund managers be seen as investing and buying business to hold for long term or trading and renting stocks? If the UT exhibits high turnover ratio, it may also mean the managers are unsure of their internal stock selection process, their fundamental beliefs, and how to approach their investment objectives.

Some investors are so obsessed with keeping costs as low as possible that they will select UTs with no sales charges, the lowest AER and the lowest platform charges. Although this attitude towards investing is admirable, I also believe in paying for results. If engaging a FAR can potentially get you additional 2% p.a. returns at the costs of 1% p.a. wrap advisory fee versus performing your own investments and spending a lot of time doing research, most investors would rather pay a small fee to get a professional to do it for them. If there are no apparent benefits that the representative has brought to the table even after three to four years, then it is time to look for another representative. Do not settle for mediocre returns. Aim for something more because your retirement and other goals are at stake.

"Past performance is not an indication of future performance" and the investor must question if, going forward, the factors and conditions that caused the UT to perform are still present, and for how long. Also, can the potential returns continue to outweigh the increased risks as the NAV is higher now and cover the total expenses of the UT?

4.2.3 Core vs tactical investments and respective holdings during different market phases

To have a dream portfolio and make consistent returns in all the four market phases (Recovery, Expansion, Crisis, Recession; *see* chapter 10.1.2) , investors need to understand what is their own personal *core* portfolio and investment strategy as opposed to *tactical* portfolio and investment strategy. Core investments are passive long-term holdings/investment mix or strategy within the investor's comfort zone; you hold these in a normal market. Tactical investments are are active short-term investment mix or strategy used to take advantage of market conditions or outlook of certain sector or geographical investments or investment themes. Therefore market monitoring and timing is more crucial in making tactical investments.

Nobody can predict how long each phase will be; it depends on a variety of reasons like what the three key parties in the economy (government, companies and individuals) are doing (*see* section 5.3), what caused the last recession, etc. I will use the duration of a soccer match to share how I would give a good estimate of how far we are into the current phase. If a normal soccer match is 90 minutes long, we can ask ourselves: Given all information on hand, are we at the early stage (15 mins to 40 mins), middle stage (40 mins to 60 mins) or late part of the phase (60 mins to 90 mins)? Then we take appropriate action. I started with 15 mins because by the time we can reasonably spot and confirm that the phase has indeed shifted into the next, we are already at least weeks or even a couple of months into the phase already.

A general core and tactical portfolio can be suggested according to current phase of the market and where investors foresee the markets will head in the next two to three years after consulting with their FAR. With this big picture, FARs can customise the percentage holdings within each type of UT according to the investor's risk profile, investment horizon, investment objectives, etc. The UTs in brackets in the following section are UTs that I personally like as my core holdings, and I will also include a tactical strategy and holdings. Of course, I wish to highlight again that every investor is a unique individual with different investment beliefs, so please use this only as a guide and customise the percentage of each UT and strategy to your liking.

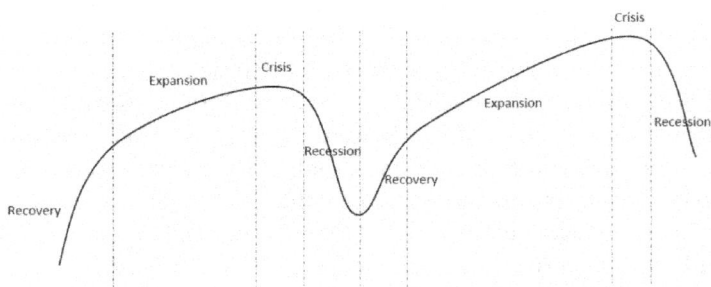

Recovery

Core strategy – Regular investing via deduction of UT holdings (*see* section 6.2.4) out of MM and bonds UTs into high yield bonds, regional/single country equity and sector UTs. Investors can add ad hoc lump sum into equity and sector UTs after clearer signs/data and news that markets had bottomed out. The lump sum is saved from many months of suspending RSP investments from the previous recession phase.

Core holdings –Trim and rebalance out MM UTs (Phillip MM fund) and high-grade Bond funds (United SGD Fund) to increase single country equity UT (Aberdeen Singapore Equity), regional equities UTs (First State Dividend Advantage). Investors may also want to add some high yield bonds UT (Aviva

Investors Global High Yield Bond) into their portfolio as most central banks would have slashed interest rates or kept it low at this juncture to spur growth. Thus high yield bond prices are expected to appreciate further. Furthermore, because the market have just moved from the previous recessionary phase, companies in the recovery phase face less credit risk of going bankrupt, which is a good news for high yield bonds UT.

Tactical Strategy and holdings–Investors with a higher risk appetite may want to invest lump sum in emerging markets single country UTs (Aberdeen Thailand Equity or Aberdeen Indonesia Equity) or regional emerging markets equities (Aberdeen Global Emerging Markets) as their magnitude of rebound is usually greater since developing market equities typically drop more than developed markets in the recession phase. They may also invest lump sum into sector UTs with heavy exposure to financials (JP Morgan Global Financials Fund), consumer discretionary (Amundi Global Luxury and Lifestyle fund) and IT (Henderson Global Technology).

Expansion

Core strategy–Continue investing in equities. Start regular savings monthly investment plan by RSP via UT holdings or monthly giro as there will likely be a lot of volatility in the expansionary phase of the market.

Core holdings–Regional equities of developing countries (Legg Mason WA Southeast Asia Special Situations) and developed countries (Fidelity America fund UT) typically do well in the expansionary phase of the economy, although not delivering as spectacular returns as the recovery phase.

Tactical Strategy and holdings–In the expansionary phase, investors can shift more allocation to UTs with a heavier focus on IT (Henderson Global Technology) and Industrials (Schroder Global Smaller Companies Fund). Investors with a higher risk appetite can also increase their UT portfolio to add energy and materials holdings (First State Global Resources).

Crisis

Core strategy–Take profit and keep cash. Rebalance and switch out of all categories of UT into MM and high grade bonds UTs. Put on hold and suspend all RSP strategies.

Core holdings–Hold only MM and high grade bonds UT. Liquidate or switch out high yield bond and equities UTs.

Tactical Strategy and holdings–Maintain same as core strategy. It is advisable for investors who are still holding on to UT with heavy allocation to energy and materials sector to start liquidating or switching their entire holdings into MM UTs. Even though their drop initially in the first one to two months of the recession phase is not as drastic plunge as other sectors and other equity UTs, it will only be a matter of time before energy and materials UTs plunge sharply; as sales and factory production fall so will the demand for energy and materials drop too.

Recession

Core strategy–If the portfolio has earlier been switched and is now taking shelter in MM and high grade bonds UT, congratulations! Keep a close tab on the economic/financial news and the unfolding of fiscal (like reduction of interest rates) and monetary policies (increasing money supply or bond buy-back policies by central banks) and their effects on the financial markets. If the investor feels that the markets have more or less bottomed out, he/she can adopt the core and tactical strategies discussed for Recovery phase.

Core holdings–Continue to hold MM UTs (Phillip MM fund) and high grade short duration Bond funds (United SGD Fund).

Tactical Strategy and holdings–At this time of writing, there is not many UTs available in Singapore that can profit from recessionary markets, other than a few Hedge fund UTs (Man AHL SGD Trend) that can take short positions and potentially make money in a prolonged recession. Fund managers of most UTs in Singapore invest with a buy-and-hold strategy and adopt long positions in their holdings.

If the investor also has a representative assisted wrap account, I advise regular yearly or bi-yearly reviews with the FAR or whenever there are any changes to their investment objectives, risk profiles, etc., or when the markets are turbulent and they feel very insecure and uncertain of their investments. The representative's role is to suggest a course of action to chart, or UTs to switch to respond to the markets. Ask questions like: how many years have the representative been in this industry? In terms of profits/losses where do most of his/her clients stand? What is his/her approach to investing UTs? Most importantly how the representative is going to add value to me.

When I speak to some investors, I am surprised that most of them are not close to their representatives or have not met up for quite a while. Regular meetings are important to foster good communication and to align and affirm the representative's advice is still congruent with the investor.

Never settle for less than you deserve. Demand the best, accept nothing less, always work with the 'A' team professionals in selecting UTs and choose the most appropriate representative who understands you and works in your best interest during the investment. It will be a bonus if they are your best pal or relative, but sometimes close relations may not be the best people when it comes to money matters and management and relations may turn sour. Do not hesitate to switch funds or change representative if there are no apparent benefits or value added after a couple of years. Remember that one of the ingredients for compounding of returns is time; and time once lost, is lost forever.

4.2.4 Ample diversification for risk management

One important tip is to diversify well and build a complete portfolio so investments can survive financial catastrophes. Do not be overexposed to any single asset class, or sector or country. For example, holding a majority of tech stocks during the dot.com bubble burst in 2000 would have been disastrous. The Nasdaq closed at 5,048.62 points on 10 March 2000 before it crashed; it took over 15 years until April 2015 to recover and close at 5,056.06 points on 23 April 2015. Another example is Japanese equities from 1990 to 2012 (the lost decades). Investors who concentrated their wealth into technology counters and Japanese equities and bought them during their peak would also have lost decades of opportunity to compound their wealth. We should consider UTs with diversifying geography, sectors, investment style and growth potential.

The table below is my recommendation for the maximum allocation into other UT categories (explained more in chapter 9) according to the investor's risk profile. My personal rule of thumb is to never invest 100% of your capital into any one category of UTs, except during periods of crisis or recession, when it is feasible to take shelter in MM and short duration bonds UTs. Generally, however, for diversification, you should not allocate 100% of your capital in any category, even for investors with high risk appetite. Some categories of UT (e.g., alternatives, thematic and sector) can be totally avoided if the investors are unfamiliar or not optimistic on their growth.

UT Categories	Low-Risk investors	Medium-Risk investors	High-Risks investors
Money Markets	70–100%	50–100%	30–100%
Short duration high grade Bonds	80–100%	60–100%	40–100%
High Yield	≤15%	≤25%	≤35%
Balanced	≤15%	≤25%	≤35%
Alternatives	≤5%	≤10%	≤20%
Regional Equities	≤15%	≤25%	≤35%
Single Country equities	≤10%	≤20%	≤30%
Thematic	≤5%	≤10%	≤20%
Sector	≤5%	≤15%	≤25%

The sector UT maximum of ≤25% for high risk investor is on a per sector basis so if the investor is optimistic on both commodity sector and healthcare sector, I would suggest, he invests not more than 25% of his total investment capital in each sector UT, the same goes for regional equities at ≤35% per region.

4.2.5 Reinvestment and rebalancing to stay in line with your investment philosophy and objectives as we progress through life stages

Most of us have a working lifespan of between 35 to 50 years depending on when we start working and when we retire. So I will divide our working lives into three stages and assume a corresponding general risk appetite. Of course, there are exceptions and I have met fresh graduates who are extremely risk averse and only want capital protected or very safe investments and retirees in their sixties whom have an aggressive stance towards investing. We can use this table below as a general guide:

UT Categories	Early stage (first 10 years)	Middle Stage (mid 20–25 years)	Late (last 5 to 15 years)
Money Markets	30–100%	50–100%	70–100%
Short duration high grade Bonds	40–100%	60–100%	80–100%
High Yield	≤35%	≤25%	≤15%
Balanced	≤35%	≤25%	≤15%
Alternatives	≤20%	≤10%	≤5%
Regional Equities	≤35%	≤25%	≤15%
Single Country equities	≤30%	≤20%	≤10%
Thematic	≤20%	≤10%	≤5%
Sector	≤25%	≤15%	≤5%
Reinvestment of dividends	**Definitely Yes**	Yes	**Depends**

As we progress through different life stages, the emphasis highlighted above is to rebalance our long-term strategic investment allocation slowly to hold more bonds and MM UT. It is important to note core allocation should take priority within each life stage should there be market opportunities during recovery, expansionary phase or threats in crisis and recession phases, then we can make some tactical adjustments and investments.

In the first one third of working life, one is still relatively young and does not have much experience of investments and the markets. There are fewer housing mortgage repayments, family obligations and costs. The priority is often to quickly pay off study loans and not get into credit card debt. With any surplus monies, I firmly believe that young people should buy insurance to protect their future unearned income stream in the event of a premature death, disability or critical illness, which would result in not able to work until late stage of one's working life. This age group is in the mid-twenties to mid-thirties (first third of our working life) and insurance premiums are more affordable as their health conditions are better and hence are more insurable. Many clients tell me that this is the stage where they have the health and time, but do not have much wealth.

For investments during this early working stage, investors can afford to be more aggressive and have as much as 70–80% of investments in equities UT (section 9.6–9.8) and the remainder in bonds/MM or balanced UTs (section 9.1–9.4) as we have the luxury of time to make back any losses. Even if younger investors lose money investing, they should gain lessons and practical knowledge to move on and make their next investment better. Although it is never a good feeling to lose money, the silver lining is that it is better now versus when investors are older with more wealth and bigger investment capital. Using the analogy of learning to ride a bicycle, most readers who know how to ride a bicycle would be thankful we fell down and pick ourselves up while we are young versus learning to ride only in our sixties with brittle bones.

As investors move on to the second third of their working life, they have a bit more wealth from having worked for over 15 years. They still have their health but probably not have the time to track and manage the investments due to the work, having assumed managerial and supervisory roles. This is also the sandwiched class, who have to take care of family commitments in the form of both aged parents and possibly young children.

Our financial needs will likewise be sandwiched between healthcare for ageing parents, maybe saving up for university tuition for young children, and our own retirement in the next 15–20 years too. Investors need to be more cautious with their investments, so I recommend a 50% equity UT and 50% bonds/ MM UT portfolio. A balanced investment is good as we do not know when we may suddenly need to liquidate the investments due to unforeseen medical expenses incurred by dependents. They should consider buying medical insurance for their dependents; parents with more financial means can consider whole life insurance plans to give their young children a head start.

Lastly in the final third of our working life and into retirement, I advise placing about 70% or more of the investment assets in short duration high grade bonds UT and MM UT, and the balance in equities UT as the core portfolio. This is the stage where most people have wealth and more time if they are about to retire, but may be lacking in health.

Investors at this stage should adopt a more cautious approach to their investments as they do not have the youth, energy or health to make back the capital they might lose in their investments, even if they have over 30 years of investment wisdom. This composition is good if they are forced to liquidate their instruments if there are any health scares (themselves or their loved ones).

For UT dividends, it is highly encouraged during the early and middle stage to re-invest them to purchase more units as most platforms do not charge sales charge on dividend reinvestments. Investors can compound their returns with the reinvested dividends over time; reinvesting UTs with monthly/quarterly dividend payout can also reap the good benefits of dollar cost averaging. This is like delayed gratification to cash out the dividends only when we are fully retired. For investors wanting to have the luxury to choose an early retirement, I encourage them to live within their means, or even better below their means, and re-invest part of their pay raise and bonus regularly from an early working stage. Many older clients told me that it matters more how much the person is able to save more than how much the person is able to earn, and if they can turn back the clock, they will choose to be a more ferocious saver.

Key learning points

- Be crystal clear on your own investment objectives before investing

- Do not over-trust the FAR. Check the FAR's background and ask to be shown quantifiable proofs of what the FAR claims

- Avoid herd mentality, either chasing returns of yesteryear's top performers or trying to time the market and follow the footsteps of others blindly

- Avoid being over conservative (put all our money in bank accounts) or over gung-ho and greedy in taking risks in our investments (use leverage excessively)

- Monitor all investments regularly. Ignorance is not bliss!

- Everyone who works hard for their money deserves to have their dream investment portfolio to also work hard for them

- Select a UT manager with an investment style that is congruent and comfortable for you

- Be mindful of fees and charges and weigh them against actual benefits and potential benefits

- Understand what is your unique comfortable core (long term) and tactical (short term) investments and their respective percentage holdings in our portfolio during different stages of the market cycle

- Have ample diversification for risk management

- Remember to re-invest dividends, pay increments, bonuses and to rebalance your portfolio to stay in line with your investment philosophy and objectives as you progress through different life stages

Endnotes

10. There is a free risk questionnaire https://www.cpf.gov.sg/cpf_info/ie/IE_Risk.asp online.
11. www.mas.gov.sg
12. You can use this website to check: https://masnetsvc2.mas.gov.sg/drr/rr.do
13. One way to do this is to look at the current NAV vs all-time high, all-time low, plus 1-year high, 3-years high etc.

5

Emotional and Psychological States of Investors

Warren Buffett's mentor Benjamin Graham once said that the stock market in the long term is a weighing machine, but in the short term is a voting machine. This is because in the long term businesses with good fundamentals and true value will reflect these qualities in their share price. In the short term, there will be erratic fluctuations in their share price because of the 'noise' generated by investors whose investment decisions are influenced by their emotions.

This chapter tracks the majority of investors (the Passives) and the second and more savvy group of investors (the Proactives) at different stages of a UT investment and imagines their corresponding thoughts and emotions. Through this, we can understand and control our emotions to become better investors.

5.1 Pre-Investment

Yes! I just got my bonus, I just got a promotion, I just received a maturity sum for my endowment plan, I want to follow my friend whom made 10% in just a week, etc. At any moment, there are hundreds of reasons for people to want to invest, which is a better decision compare to splurging on extravagant luxury items or even a trip to the casino.

Some Passives will invest with the herd mentality, following the advice of their friends, colleagues or brokers who may claim to possess superior information or insider news. Others will follow the celebrity investors on TV or the radio. There are also Singaporeans who merely wanted to perform a simple bank transaction at the branch office, but ended up becoming a UT investor when the banker or relationship manager came over to 'speak' to him/her.

What would Proactives consider before investing? Of the three stages of investing, I believe the pre-investment stage is most critical. Proactives would ask questions about the suitability of the UT for himself/herself. The more questions asked, and more research and homework done before investing, the lesser the magnitude of emotions and irrational behaviour playing a part in the investment decision later on.

The most important question most Proactives ask is, " Do I understand the investment?" It is followed by, " What is it about, which geographical area and main sectors is it investing in, how is the UT being managed by the fund manager, what are the merits of the UT if I invest now, what are the risk factors that I foresee will impact this investment, can I accept and tolerate the risks, what are my maximum losses, what are the fees and charges?" Finally the question that differentiates Proactives from the Passives, " Do I really need to invest? What can I do if I do not invest the monies?"

Despite enticing discounted upfront fees, shopping vouchers, past performance indicators, or seeing statement of accounts of other investors who had invested in the same UT earlier and made money, every investor needs to learn to keep their emotions of greed and fear of loss in check at this stage and not be enticed to just jump in. He or she must still independently make the decision on the suitability of the UT.

I like to stress at this point that if the investor has thought about all the previous questions and wishes to proceed with the investment, it will also be good to look at the performance history and track record of the UT, especially one that shows as long a horizon as possible charted out so they get an understanding of how the UT behaves and performs during the four different market cycles (recovery, expansion, crisis, recession discussed earlier). Even though most disclaimers will indicate that past performance is not indicative of future results, it does not hurt to look at the past chart patterns to form a better understanding before investing.

5.2 During the Investment

I have identified 15 different emotions that investors may experience through the time period of any investment, including UTs. These emotions correspond with the market cycle and value of their investments. It is possible for investors to experience overlapping emotions of two or even three states at any one time. As the intensity of the thoughts and emotions are in line with the market cycles and the UT performance, this may varies between individuals as a paper loss of $10,000 could mean 10% for someone with net investible assets of $100,000 but only 1% for another investor with $1 million to invest. The thoughts and emotions in brackets should be the feelings that a savvy and prudent investor or an investor with a good, dedicated representative might experience at the 15 stages.

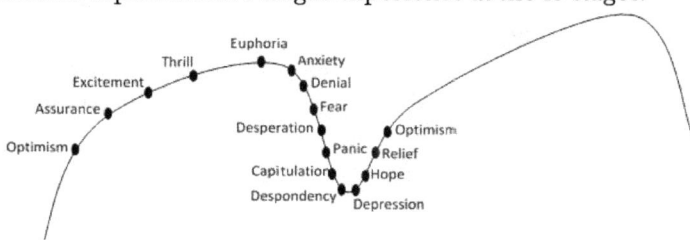

5.2.1 Optimism

Passives have just confirmed the trade and are hopeful that the investment will break even on the charges quickly.

Proactives are feeling confident at this point as they have done their homework on the investment and the markets at the pre-investment stage.

5.2.2 Assurance

Passives have just broken even on the initial sales charges. Any upward gains beyond this point are profits. They feel reassured.

Proactives know that doing their homework has paid off and the investment has broken even; there is likely more upside potential, although they are not complacent and look again at the changes in the factsheet of the UT and also tune in to daily market news.

5.2.3 Excitement

Passives are feeling excited: they are seeing real profits now. The UT closes higher and higher week by week, there are more days the UT close in the green than in the red. Passives starts to think, "If I had known beforehand I would have bought more units", and may feel a small tinge of regret for investing such a small amount. Passives might even contemplate increasing the investment and buying more units at this stage. Some go around telling friends and colleagues about their investments gains.

Proactives are proven right again! Their investments have grown and they are sitting on paper gains of high single digits or low double digits. They are delighted but at the same time also increasingly cautious and check developed and developing countries news to see signs of inflationary pressures and watch out for announcement of interest rates hike from central banks all over the world.

5.2.4 Thrill

Yes! Passives wake up happy every other day, especially when they view their investment portfolio online. They start to think highly of their investment acumen and hope that their daily investment profits will one day be higher than their daily salary. At this point, the 'If I had' syndrome comes back again with greater intensity. They will recall how, a few weeks or months ago, they contemplated increasing the investment, but did not. They will be thinking 'if I had' increased the UT investments then, the UTs would have broke even and maybe making profits. Some investors, for fear of missing out on more upside, will quickly purchase more UTs.

The Proactives portfolios are showing double digit gains and even over 20% paper gains. They are increasingly getting nervy as they recall one of Wall Street's famous saying in the 1910s: "No trees grow to the sky." Most prudent investors will at this point take 30% to 70% of the profits and switched to MM and short duration bonds UT. The percentage varies for each investor's individual risk appetite, outlook of the market and other factors. This group of investors or advised by good FARs will not likely buy more UTs now.

5.2.5 Euphoria

Every day is rosy at this point, even the birds are chirping, traffic is smoother. Passives feel energetic and everything seems perfect. Their childrens' university plans and their own retirement plans are all on track. If the investments continue to grow at this rate, Passives might dream of firing their boss soon. It seems to be easy money; they might continue to add more units to their investments to increase their total profit.

This is known as the point of maximum financial gain and also maximum financial risk and the best time to exit the markets, since absolutely no one can predict the highest and best closing day prior to a recession without a crystal ball. The Proactives get so edgy at this point they switch out 80% to 100% of their riskier UTs, equity and balanced UTs to short duration bonds or MM UT and in some cases sell all their UTs. They only feel euphoric if they have completed the switch and realised the profits.

5.2.6 Anxiety

Ok, there is some minor pullback and correction, it is normal to have some bad news in the financial markets. Passives wait and see. Some of the their gains have eroded, but overall their portfolio is still in the black.

Proactives look into their reliable fear gauge/index also known as the Chicago Board Options Market Volatility index (VIX) for past movements and the magnitude for the last 30 days. If they do not like the volatility or do not feel good, they will switch out all their remaining UTs into MM and short duration bonds and await more news and direction. For proactives that still want to hold equity UT, most would have switched to UTs with heavier weight on consumer staples, utilities and telcos at this point.

5.2.7 Denial

More bad news for the markets to digest. Markets close in the red for three to four days out of five dealing days in the week. There might still be some profit to be made, but it is nothing compared to just a few months back.

Passives think they should maybe still hold on to their positions and pray that markets will U-Turn. In denial, they do not see the bigger picture of a major correction and most economies that are about to enter a recession.

Proactives would have recognised most signs that economies are entering a bear market phase. It seems to be early bear just moving out of the cave, so they will be observing and adopt a wait-and-see stance. Proactives who are more savvy and gung-ho at this point will look at instruments or alternative UTs that can short the market or buy put options, which will gain a profit when markets nosedive.

5.2.8 Fear

Even more grim news. Some of the experts and analyst start warning of tough times ahead and caution investors to wait before they invest, injecting more fear into the markets. Almost every day, markets close in the red, and seem to decline at a steeper rate.

Passives start to think, are we entering a bear market? The bulk of the gains have already been eroded, and now is back to square one. Passives' losses might still be manageable at 15% to 30% (depend on which stage of the cycle they bought the UT). Passives starts to lose a bit of sleep and appetite, more so if they had invested with leverage, personal loans and lines of credit.

Proactives are seeing trends and signs the bear is gaining strength and the bull is on the retreat. They will continue their strategy to short the market. MM UT and short duration bonds UT categories will likely see increased funds flow into them as their prices are more stable.

5.2.8 Desperation

Passives do not even want to listen to the news or read the financial section of the papers or view their portfolio online. The losses might have compound to 30% to 60% by now. They start to feel desperate and decide to wait for the next few days before making a decision. Some passives might think of selling off their entire portfolio now and realise the loss, others may feel the storm will pass eventually as they continue to hold, after all, as long as they do not sell it is only a loss on paper. They may get angry and their emotions may damage their relationship with their children and spouse and work at the workplace just seems more stressful and run into more obstacles.

Proactives' profits are piling up. They are also getting increasingly cautious and watch the news twice a day to see if there are interventions by central banks or governments around the world, or if they have agreed on cohesive actions.

5.2.9 Panic

Perhaps news breaks of major corporations having problems keeping afloat. Some big MNCs with over 100 years of history file for bankruptcy. As globalization had made more companies more interdependent on each other for business and survival, like dominos, a list of companies that have been identified as having high risk and exposure and may face liquidation grabs headlines.

Passives start to panic also, their past stance of not looking at financial news or listening to the TV does not work now as the headlines dominate the front page of every major global newspaper. Many passives will exit now realising 45% to 70% losses, three quarters into the carnage. Some passives would rather accept a total write-off and admit it was a wrong decision and wrong time to invest.

Proactives can make even more money when markets nosedive through their put options and alternative UTs that can short the equities and/or index. However they also know there are no infinite plunge and even the deepest ocean also have a depth. Markets will reach a bottom and rebound up; hence they start to trim the put options amount, depending on the news and the sentiments then.

5.2.10 Capitulation

Some passives who did not sell earlier see their portfolios decline by a further 10%–15%. They will think if the bear market and sentiments continue; will there be any residual value left? Some passive that have resisted selling earlier will be desperate to sell now and are willing to sell and recover just 25% of their capital or even less. They are contented to just sell their portfolio to avoid bigger losses. They become grumpy and Murphy's Law seems to apply in all aspects of their lives.

Proactives will feel more edgy now even though they have made more money. They know markets have been depressed for so many quarters or even years and by now, the only likely way is up. Their mindset will turn and see this as a buying opportunity while most passives see doom and feel gloom. Proactives will reverse their strategy to buy certain equity UTs with very low NAVs at deep discounts; it is like a 70% clearance sale for them. They may also buy equity UTs using the DCA method in batches of lump sum investment.

5.2.11 Despondency

More passives have exited their UT investments and feel that investments are just not for them; some may even swear not to invest again. They would rather place their hard-earned monies in fixed and time deposits at least their capital is preserved.

Proactives see this stage as the point of minimum financial risk and maximum financial gain, and a rare opportunity to buy equities/businesses and UTs with good fundamentals that are heavily sold down. This great buying opportunity is rarer than the World Cup and Olympics combined and take more than eight years to come by! If they have started to purchase stocks and re-enter the market a few weeks or months ago, their minds may tell them to continue to accumulate stocks and equity UTs at a depressed price, even they may be sitting on a paper loss of 5% to 10% if they have purchased UTs earlier; they will think of averaging down their purchases. Bolder proactives may want to increase their investment amounts now.

5.2.12 Depression

As markets seem to have fewer wild swings and fluctuations, the dust settles. Many passives who have received their hardcopy statements will see losses of five figures or even six figures in their profit/loss column. Some will feel very depressed as reality hits, others will calculate how many months of bonuses were wiped out and how many years of savings they have to put aside to make back their losses. Some passives that were originally near their retirement age now have to extend their working life and delay their retirement for a few more years.

Proactives will recognise that markets are stabilising. They will completely reverse any put or short positions on the market and start to switch to a long investment strategy with optimistic outlook on the markets, and increase their earlier investments in batches while waiting for more news of an economic turnaround.

5.2.13 Hope

For the passives who did not sell their investments earlier despite feelings of fear, desperation and panic, the day has finally come where there is a daily increase in buying activity on the stock exchanges. Prices have more or less been more stable in the recent weeks. These passives now feel hopeful.

Proactives feel vindicated. Their decision to reverse their investment strategy and invest long in the market has paid off. They are able to see markets close on average 2% to 3% higher week on week and their investments break even very fast. At this point, the proactives will add more securities and UTs in bigger quantities to their portfolio as they recognise it is now the early days of the recovery phase.

5.2.14 Relief

Markets seem to be finally making a U-Turn. Investors who started buying equities UT a couple of months back will also feel relief. Exchanges are closing higher and passives that held on earlier can see their portfolio values growing rapidly and feel relief that their losses are getting smaller. Some passives will contemplate new investments and start buying equity UTs.

Proactives will continue to pick up more stocks, and equity UTs as global interest rates are still low and other signs governments are helping companies and repairing the economies. Other investors might still be reeling in despair and sadness of how much they have lost in the previous recession, and also the missed opportunity of buying in at the market low a few months ago to capitalise on the spectacular recovery they have seen. This is the middle of the recovery period and growth momentum is picking up steam, with buying volumes higher than selling volumes. Many of the big institutional buyers and investors have returned to the market to purchase stocks and UTs. They have seen solid growth in the past couple of months and the market consensus is that the worst is already over.

5.2.15 Optimism

The cycle of human emotions and thoughts repeats itself again with the market cycle. Being human, some investors have already forgotten the previous panic and fear; others have been scarred so deeply they will never consider investing again. Yet others have learnt their lessons well and emerge from the recession as a more rational and savvy investor. The last group will henceforth think like a Proactive in the future.

This table summarises the 15 emotions discussed and common mistakes investors may make as well as practical steps I advise at each stage of the investment cycle.

Emotions	Common mistakes	Practical steps
Optimism	Most investors do not do enough homework and ask themselves the questions raised in the pre-investment section.	Investors should research online for the UTs they have shortlisted and also speak to 1 or 2 FARs if they deemed the investment amount to be a big % of their surplus.
Assurance	Some investors rejoice after breaking even, grow complacent and do not check their UT performance at all.	Investors should continue to check their portfolio once every 3–5 days and stay alert and updated on daily business and market news that may affect their UTs.
Excitement	Investors might think of investing more capital at the current higher price since they have broke even.	Investors should monitor the news closely more now than the previous stage to watch out for early signs of governments tightening the economy especially raising interest rates, raising bank's reserve ratio, reducing loan quantum to income for borrowers, etc.
Thrill	Many investors start to feel greedy and will want to increase their investments thinking that it is easy money.	Investors should examine their portfolio more closely and look at their UTs with the most exposure to equities or in countries and regions where there has been confirmed news of governments wanting to contract the economy to switch out a portion to bonds and MM UTs.
Euphoria	Some investors still want to chase after higher returns and get consumed by greed. They fail to see that most equity markets have Price/earnings > 30 and NAV of equity UTs are setting new all time high levels and typically 25–40% higher than the previous crisis.	Investors should switch out their equity UTs to bonds and MM UTs at a pace faster than the previous thrill emotion. This is the calm before the storm and they must not be greedy and know when to take profit and exit.
Anxiety	Many investors do not see it as the first wave before subsequent bigger waves that a financial tsunami is about to hit and still continue to hold on to their equity UTs.	Investors should just take profit despite the UTs being 5%-8% lower than their all-time high a couple of weeks ago. They must not be greedy and unrealistic to anticipate the markets will recover to its previous high without intervention so soon.
Denial	Many investors still commit the mistake of not selling their equity UTs. They hold on, praying for the markets to recover.	Investors should pay close attention to the news and majority of the views of analyst/experts. They can also take reference from the VIX index. Even If all their previous profits are gone and they are back to square one with only their capital, it is still advisable to switch out their equity UTs.

Fear	The common mistake that investors make at this point is to be unwilling to accept losing 15% to 30% of their capital; This causes them to hold on to a losing investment longer than they should.	Although it is painful to recognise losing 15–30% of the capital, it is still possible to switch out of equity UTs as long as there is still >70% of the capital, the investor must recognise and understand they can still invest later on when markets are even lower.
Desperation	Many investors make the mistake of feeling attached to their investments and refuse to acknowledge the financial news. Some may commit the mistake of feeling regretful and think back a few weeks or months ago, they did not sell their UTs and now it has dropped by a further 15–30%, they become more reluctant to sell.	Although the investor may only get back 50% of their capital. They should still bite the bullet and switch to lower risk bonds and MM UTs at this juncture if the general consensus is that turbulent times are ahead.
Panic	Fear and panic overpower investor's previous emotions of denial and regret of losses. Some of them will give in and sell their equities UT at losses of 45–70% three quarters through the carnage.	The decision to sell or switch now may come too late as most investors head for the exits. If investors have kept to one of the golden rule of investing at the start: Only invest with monies one can afford to lose. Now would be a good time to start investing in equities UT with their surpluses.
Capitulation	At this stage, more investors will give in to the selling pressure. Stress and negative emotions cloud their rationale judgement. Even recovering 15–25% of their capital, they will still sell.	Investors should try to remain calm and look through their UT portfolio again. Examine their investment objectives and top 10 holdings, etc. Instead of selling, they can start buying more units of UTs with good fundamentals in their top 10 holdings to reduce their unit price of investment and adopt 'averaging down' technique.
Despondency	At this point, some investors will still continue to sell their UTs although there is lesser gloomy news of companies in trouble compared to the previous two stages. There is also fresh news as governments are coming together to discuss a collective plan and course of action although it is yet to be finalised.	At this point, we are 80–90% through the recession. This is the worse time to sell the equities UT. Investors should start to rebalance their UT allocation to switch out from their bonds and MM UTs into equities UT or invest their surplus cash/CPF savings/SRS into equities UT.

Depression	Investors that sold earlier and not invested back in the markets are still reeling from shock. Some may be so permanently scarred they vow against all forms of investments.	To feel shock, demoralised, cheated, etc is all normal. The faster investors can get over these feelings and pull themselves and get their act together and look at present opportunities in the market when current NAV of some equities UTs are only a third or lesser of their all time highs. This is a wonderful time to buy equities UT. I suggest the best medicine to cure this depression would be to make even more money again this time from the recovery market phase.
Hope	At this stage, investors have seen markets behaving more normally and NAV of their equities UT posting mid to high single digit growth month on month. Some investors make the mistake of taking profits too early.	This is the turnaround sign. Even though equities UT prices are climbing rapidly, investors can and should still jump on the bandwagon to switch their holdings to more equities UT if they have not done so previously as there is still plenty of room for upside and hold to them longer unless the UT objectives changes and not to be too hasty to take profit.
Relief then back to Optimism	At this stage, investors who sold off their equities UT and vowed not to invest again might regret missing out on the early months of the spectacular recovery; they still want to sit on the sidelines waiting for an opportunity or for prices to drop to levels of the depression stage.	These investors must remember the wise saying: No point crying over spilled milk. Even if they missed the earlier opportunity a couple of months back or they lost a fair bit of their capital many months ago, they should still start accumulating more equities UT as this is likely to be the early-mid recovery phase and there is still the expansionary phase for equities UT to continue to do well.

5.3 Before disposing of the investment

Investors can sell off their UTs at any point during the 15 stages. I just want to have a separate section here to let readers consider some of these points before they sell off their investments the next time. Most investors will be thinking of how much they have made, and if it is enough to cover the upfront sales charge. Some investors will consider if it is the wrong move; perhaps that particular UT is the starlet in their investment portfolio and selling it off would be like killing their golden goose.

Investors must be wary of their greed at this stage. A 1% net profit is always better than a loss. They should not think about their past paper gains being higher than now if their positions are realised and not to sell off their UTs. For investors to cut their losses, we can refer to the saying: "He who fights and runs away, lives to fight another day". So even if we were to lose 10% to 20% of our capital if we sell the UTs, we should still do it and wait for another opportunity to reinvest back in the market. As long as investors are not left with anything less than 20% of his/ her original capital and the spirit of investing is still alive, the investor can still make a comeback in the future.

Just before disposing of their investments, investors should ask themselves some questions. For example, at which stage of the economy are we already in? (*See* section 4.2.3 for the football match duration example.) Is it more likely for my UTs to appreciate further, going forward into the next phase of the economic cycle? What are the three parties (government, companies and consumers) in the economy doing: is the government printing more money and making credit easy for consumers and supporting the companies to restore confidence and repair the economy, or is the government taking measures to tighten and curb further economic growth? It is uncommon for all three parties to be simultaneously spending and spending excessively for prolonged periods in the economy, as increased government spending may have a 'crowding-out' effect causing companies not to be able to spend or invest as they are competing for resources against the government's spending.

Knowing what the three parties are doing at any point of time in the economy can help the investor plan ahead to shift and rebalance the current percentage allocation of MM, Bonds and Equity UT in their portfolio and make a more informed, rational decision of what and when to sell. If the government is spending on public projects and having very loose monetary and fiscal policies, it is likely the economy is still in the recovery and early expansionary phase, and companies and consumers are not spending so much. This is still generally a good time to buy equity UTs as the loose policies are to spur economic growth and will help companies deliver better bottom lines and nudge the share price up.

In the middle expansionary to crisis stage, companies' balance sheets have already improved tremendously companies are starting to expand; they reinvest their machinery and capital expenditure, bid more projects and hire more workers. Consumers will spend more as they are more optimistic of their job prospects and future as the unemployment rate is very low. The companies and consumers will have increased their spending and governments would already have reduced their spending and possibly started to raise interest rates and deploy other contracting monetary and fiscal policies to control and slow down the rate of growth. This will be the time to start increasing the percentage of the investment portfolio into MM UTs and short duration bonds UT and reduce all other categories of UTs generally.

In the recession stage, consumers reduce their spending as they read more news of retrenchments and companies going bankrupt. Likewise, companies will be careful in their spending as their sales have slowed due to reduced spending and consumption of goods by consumers. Companies may also start to lay off workers in view of the recession ahead. The government will step in when they feel the economy has contracted enough and will cut interest rates, employ other fiscal and monetary tools to spur growth, and ramp up spending, give subsidies to companies, try to save jobs, and make financing accessible to businesses. At the late recession stage, investors should sell off MM and bonds UT to reallocate their capital into equity UTs, high yields UTs and balanced UTs.

Another reason the current actions of the three parties (government, companies and consumers) are important and will affect the value of investments and UT prices because we know in an economy:

- GDP = C + I + G +(X-M)
- C= Consumption, I= Net Investments, G= Government spending, and (X-M) = Net Exports.

Excessive spending for C, I and G for prolonged periods will lead to a high GDP, which may result in overheating in the economy. Overheating in the economy will lead to subsequent long periods of mild and lower than average economic growth that Central Banks try to avoid (reminds us of China's double digit GDP from the 1990s to 2007 and the current 7.5% GDP growth rate the Chinese government wants after 2012.). Overheating causes demand pull inflation as increased competition for scarce resources like manpower and machinery production will make locally produced goods more expensive and not sellable overseas, reducing the economy's exports revenue.

Central banks will respond to overheated economies[14] and prevent excessive high levels of inflation either by raising interest rates to make borrowing and leverage expensive to reduce consumption and corporate spending, or by increasing every bank's capital adequacy ratio, limiting borrowers' loan-to-income ratios, etc. before the bubble becomes even bigger. Higher interest rates may encourage higher savings and lesser consumption; if consumption reduces drastically, companies will sell fewer goods and services, leading to weaker sales and hiring, wage increment freezes and layoffs. This usually leads to a period of recession in the economy before balance is achieved once more.

Singapore's MAS also adopt a series of measures rapidly after seeing potential signs of overheating especially in the property sector and decide to step in with a few rounds of cooling measures from February 2010 with the additional buyer's and seller's stamp duty, reducing the loan to value for second property that an individual can borrow, etc. Investors will benefit if they know how to analyse these measures and interpret the effects on their investments; they will want to see if they are invested in single sector property UTs in Singapore and note that UTs with companies in the top 10 holdings that are suppliers to these property developers will also likely suffer . This prompts investors to switch to other regional equity UT or a Singapore UT that has low weight on the property sector once the cooling measures are first announced.

Key learning points

- Investors emotions and psychological states can be divided into three stages: a) Pre investment (which is most important), b) During investment and c) Just before disposing the investment

- I have listed more than ten common questions that the investor should consider before investing. There may be more for different individuals. The more carefully plan out and research done will reduce the magnitude of emotions and irrational behaviours during the investment stage

- There are 15 emotional states that the investor might go through, especially during volatile and turbulent markets. I have listed possible actions one group of investors might think and take and what another different group of savvy investors might think and react.

- I have listed common mistakes that many investors may commit during each of the 15 emotional stage due to stress or being complacent, and the practical steps that they should take instead.

- Just before disposing of the UTs, investors can ask what stage of the economy we are in, going forward to the next phase, are there still room for my UTs to appreciate further? They should also ask what actions the three parties in the economy (consumers, companies and governments) are currently doing.

Endnotes

14. Some signs of this include the government raising interest rates or increasing bank's capital adequacy ratio and limit their loans to deposit ratio they can loan out, etc.

PART 2

Practice

6

How to Buy Unit Trusts

Now that you know about UTs and the advantages of investing in them, we will move on to the basics of how to start investing in UT. I am sceptical when people talk about how good they are at timing the market. Personally, I would rather learn the disciplined, rational ways to invest in UT based on which stage of the economy we are in and heading towards. For now, I will discuss the different ways to buy UT.

6.1 Lump sum

Lump sum investing is the most common way for investors to buy UT in Singapore. Most-open ended UTs sold in Singapore only require a minimum initial lump sum of $1,000. The SHK Recovery fund UT so far is an exception with hedge fund strategies and requires as much as a $100,000 initial lump sum to start investing. Usually UTs classified as alternatives, as they use hedge funds strategy, will require a higher minimum initial investment amount ranging from S$20,000 to S$55,000.

If investors invest lump sums, one word of caution is to have surplus monies to be able to buy more units should the NAV drop significantly lower than the initial price, a strategy known as 'averaging down'. For this to make sense, investors must continue to like the UT's fundamentals, long-term prospects and the management's investment decisions and style.

6.2 Regular investing and dollar cost averaging

Another approach to buying UT is to perform regular fixed amount investing. This is called monthly investment plan (MIP) or regular savings plan (RSP). There are two keywords in MIP/RSP: monthly (frequency of investing) and regular (routinely setting aside a fixed sum of money). This is a minimum of at least $100/month per UT in Singapore. There is no lock-in period and investors can change to another UT, amend the amount, change the frequency to quarterly, etc. I personally recommend monthly plans as there will be 12 entry points to invest in the year vs only 4 for quarterly investments.

6.2.1 Dollar Cost Averaging

A RSP/MIP strategy can give investors dollar cost averaging (DCA) benefits and help smooth out the volatility of the equities market as investors do not have to time the market as much as if they invest as a lump sum. By investing a fixed amount at fixed intervals regardless of market conditions, the investor will purchase more units when markets and the economy are depressed and in a recession cycle and progressively lesser units when markets are in the expansion and crisis cycle. The benefits of DCA are widely acknowledged in many investment books and literature.

For UTs that pay dividends on a monthly, quarterly or semi-annual basis, it is possible to reinvest these dividends to buy more units of the UT. This is a powerful method of investing that combines the RSP/MIP investment with the dividends to grow the portfolio, especially since there is no sales charge for dividend reinvestment and the dividend reinvestment date in the month is likely different from the regular monthly investment buy in date. This means investors can automatically reap the benefits of DCA twice for the same UT in the same month! One word of caution is that DCA will not work for investments on a decline trend over a long term as his/her new investments will average down but the total portfolio will be worth less. DCA works better on upward trending investments with more fluctuations and volatility versus just a straight line upward investment.

Many people have the misconception that DCA adds up costs over time as the investor may be performing 12 transactions over a year vs only one transaction if he/she invests once in the year. This argument is true for stocks and securities that have a minimum transaction fee per trade; however for UTs the upfront fee is a percentage of the investment amount. Assuming the following scenario:

Investment Amount	Sales Charge	Net investment after sales charge
Peter invests $12,000 lump sum	3%	$12,000 x (100%-3%) = $11,640
Sam invests $1,000/month for next 12 mths	3%	$1,000 x (100%-3%)x 12 mths = $11,640

The other misconceived disadvantage of DCA is that if the investment runs up over 12 months, Peter who invests a lump sum at the start will make more money compared to Sam who invests a regular sum over 12 months, as his average purchase price per unit will become higher as the investment increases in value. This argument is only true if the investment is a straight upward line. Let's assume sales charge of 3% for Peter and Sam and no other charges. Peter would have [(0.97×12,000)/1(price on Jan 8)] x 1.2 (Price on Dec 8) = **$13,968** on 11,640 units. Both investment styles will yield the same net investment amounts and same charges. However, their profit/loss will be different depends on the average cost/unit of investment.

Sam would accumulate a total of 11,736.935 units vs Peter's 11,640 units. Although Sam unit's average cost is $1.0359 higher than Peter's $1.0309 ($12,000/11640 units), Sam's investments is worth more at **$14,084.32**. Because he accumulated more units than Peter's lump sum investment, he thus made a higher net profit and benefited from DCA.

Sam's investments ($1,000/mth on the 8th of every month for 12 months)

Month	Unit Price	Units Purchased	Ave total cost of units (incl sales charge)
Jan	1	970	1.0309
Feb	1.04	932.692	1.0511
Mar	1.09	889.908	1.0742
Apr	1.05	923.809	1.0763
May	1.01	960.396	1.0691
Jun	0.93	1,043.01	1.0489
Jul	0.89	1,089.88	1.0279
Aug	0.91	1,065.934	1.0157
Sept	0.92	1,054.347	1.0078
Oct	0.91	1,065.934	1.0004
Nov	1.04	932.692	1.0065
Dec	1.20	808.333	1.0224
Total/Average		**11,736.935**	**1.0359**

Unit Price

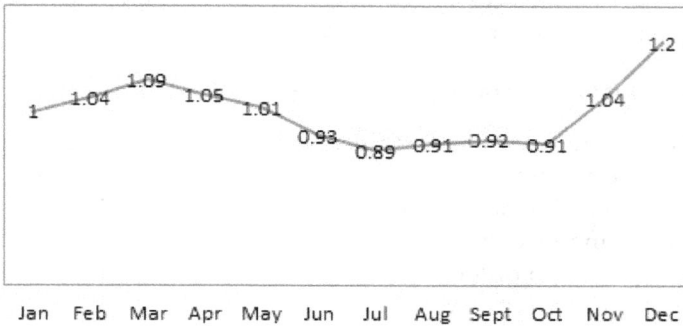

Jan Feb Mar Apr May Jun Jul Aug Sept Oct Nov Dec

We can see there were five months out of the year where the unit price of the UT fell below the initial $1 price where the investor starts the MIP/RSP, so there *need not be a prolonged period of low prices for DCA to work.*

DCA also takes the emotions out of investing as by July 8th, Peter would have suffer a paper loss of $12,000-(11,640 x 0.89) = -$1,640.4 or about -13.67%. If he had set a cut loss level of 13.5% and sold his investments, he would not have had a chance to see his investments rebound later. Compared to Sam's strategy from Jan to July 8th, he would have purchased 6,809.695 units and valued at the same $0.89, his paper loss is $7,000-(6,809.695 x 0.89) = -$939.37 or -13.41%. The loss is less compared to the lump sum investment although Sam bought units at a higher average price Jan to May.

For investments on a long-term downward trend, DCA will not work to add to the investor's wealth, however compared to an investor who invests with lump sum, at least those who invest via a DCA approach will lose less money.

iFAST is one of the distributors in Singapore that offers special RSP/MIP into selected UTs without initial investments. This means investors can get started without the $1,000 initial investment. This can be a good disciplined way for parents to teach their children who are over 21 about personal finance. They can open an investment account under their child's name, select a couple of funds to do regular investing and advise them to always pay themselves first once they get any money from holiday assignments or *angpows*, etc. The young adult will also have a longer time horizon to build their wealth if they start younger to save for their house, retirement, etc.

6.2.2 Unit Cost Averaging

The second type of MIP is Unit Cost Averaging (UCA): buying the same amount of units of the UT every month by changing the amount invested according to the UT's NAV that month. In some months, the investor must invest more when the UT's NAV goes up in order to get the same amount of units and the reverse is true.

UCA is not popular yet, as it is difficult to change the monthly investment amount every month to get the same units and most banks want a fixed giro amount monthly. It is tedious and requires discipline as the investor has to track the different investment amount every month without getting emotional. The investor may also be afraid to invest more as news may cause the UT to drop for many days and the investor will attempt to catch the lower NAV and delay the investment, thereby negating the benefit of taking emotions out of the picture through a regular investing strategy.

6.2.3 Dollar Value Averaging

Dollar Value Averaging (DVA) was developed by Harvard University Professor Michael E. Edleson in 1988. It is a combination of regular investing with varying amounts of new investments every month based on the value of the portfolio and the pre-set target. With DVA, investors contribute to their portfolio a varying amount every month so their portfolio can increase by a set amount. When markets decline, the investor contributes more and the reverse is true.

An investor that follows a DVA strategy strictly may even have periods where he/she is not required to invest for that month or be required to sell some units from their portfolio, usually when valuations are high. Thus with DVA, periods of overperformance and underperformance can be clearly tracked based on the amount of investments for that month. To put it simply *DVA synchronises concepts of DCA and portfolio rebalancing*. There is some research that concludes DVA has delivered superior performance at a similar volatility compared to the DCA method; other research refutes it.

Paul, a father, wants to set aside a sum of $50,000 in 10 years' time for his son's university education and decides to adopt a DVA investment strategy. He decides to start with an equity UT for the first seven to eight years depending on the market situation before switching to a bond UT for the last two to three years. Paul is projecting an annualised return and performance of 5% for both the equity and bond UT after charges.

Thus after meeting his financial consultant and with the help of a financial calculator to solve for PMT (Payment) [where FV = 50,000, N = 120 (10 yrs x 12 mths),I/yr = 5/12 (target rate of 5%/12 mths)], the monthly payment/savings he needs to set aside is $322. He starts investing into the UT with $332 [$322 x 1.03 for the sales charge)] every month. Before his second investment, he saw that his UT value is only $311. Thus keeping to a DVA strategy, he will now invest $322×2-$311=$333 x 1.03 sales charge = $342.99. On the third month, the value is $607. Still keeping faith with his strategy, his third investment will be $322×3-$607 x 1.03 = $369.77. Finally on the fourth month there was an equity rally and his portfolio value is $978. His fourth month fresh contribution will be $322 x 4-$978 x 1.03 = $319.3. The amount is less than his very first contribution as markets have staged a small rally and the UT's unit price is slightly more expensive now. With a DVA philosophy, he will reduce his fresh funds for investment that month and buy lesser units.

In theory, as long as the investments for the equity and bond UT delivers an average of 5% or higher per annum, Paul's target will be met as he had the discipline to add the special ingredient of $322 nett every month into his portfolio. DVA is more dynamic as it takes into account the target return and adjusts the monthly contributions accordingly versus DCA's investment approach of a regular fixed amount.

Those who benefit less from DVA are older investors who are about to retire or young investors who have a tight budget for investing every month. DVA principles require the investor to vary their investment contributions based on their portfolio values (sometimes they have to contribute 30% more than their monthly regular investment). This group of investors should use the traditional DCA method instead.

The table below summarises the concepts of DCA, UCA and DVA for a hypothetical UT (without sales charges) over a 12-month period to compare the pros and cons of the three investment methods. From the table, we can see that for UTs with volatile fluctuations in their NAV and eventually move up, DCA and UCA strategies gives better returns than DVA strategy because DVA is goal focused and requires lower investment amounts so the investor will automatically buy fewer units when the UT's NAV is high. The reverse is also true. However both the UCA method and DVA method are rigorous and require discipline and monitoring to vary the investment amount every month based on the UT's NAV.

Dollar Cost Averaging (DCA)			
Date	Investment Amt	Price	Units
Jan-14	1,000	1	1000
Feb-14	1,000	0.96	1041.66667
Mar-14	1,000	1.02	980.392157
Apr-14	1,000	1.05	952.380952
May-14	1,000	0.99	1010.10101
Jun-14	1,000	0.95	1052.63158
Jul-14	1,000	0.92	1086.95652
Aug-14	1,000	0.96	1041.66667
Sep-14	1,000	0.99	1010.10101
Oct-14	1,000	1.01	990.09901
Nov-14	1,000	1.04	961.538462
Dec-14	1,000	1.08	925.925926
Weighted Ave price/unit	12,000	1.00446	12053.46
Paper Gains/(loss) per unit = 1.08–1.00446= 0.07554			
Total Profits: 0.07554 x 12,053.46= 910.518			
% returns: 7.587%			

Unit Cost Averaging (UCA)			
Date	Investment Amt	Price	Units
Jan-14	1,000	1	1000
Feb-14	960	0.96	1000
Mar-14	1020	1.02	1000
Apr-14	1050	1.05	1000
May-14	990	0.99	1000
Jun-14	950	0.95	1000
Jul-14	920	0.92	1000
Aug-14	960	0.96	1000
Sep-14	990	0.99	1000
Oct-14	1010	1.01	1000
Nov-14	1040	1.04	1000
Dec-14	1080	1.08	1000
Weighted Ave price/unit	11,970	1.0025	12000
Paper Gains/(loss) per unit = 1.08–1.0025= 0.07749			
Total Profits: 0.07749 x 12,000= 929.92			
% returns: 7.749%			

Dollar Value Averaging			
Date	Investment Amt	Price	Units
Jan-14	1,000	1	1000
Feb-14	1,040	0.96	1083.33
Mar-14	875	1.02	857.846
Apr-14	912	1.05	868.347
May-14	1,229	0.99	1240.982
Jun-14	1,202	0.95	1265.284
Jul-14	1,189	0.92	1292.906
Aug-14	696	0.96	724.638
Sep-14	750	0.99	757.579
Oct-14	818	1.01	810.078
Nov-14	703	1.04	675.961
Dec-14	577	1.08	534.16
Weighted Ave price/unit	10,991	1.0109	11111.11
Paper Gains/(loss) per unit = 1.08-1.0109= 0.06907			
Total Profits: 0.06907 x 11,111.11= 767.466			
% returns: 6.983%			

6.2.4 Regular Savings via UT Holdings

The fourth way to buy UTs is Regular savings via UT Holdings. It is my personal favourite and is available on some investment platforms like iFAST. This requires the investor to first invest a lump sum into a low volatility short duration bond or money market (MM) UT. Units will then be deducted monthly from the short duration bond or MM UT and proceeds of the deducted units will be invested into other equity UTs to also take advantage of DCA benefits.

For example, Jack likes the idea of investing in a few equity UTs. Although he already has a lump sum to invest, he feels that current UT prices are a little high. Therefore he can start with an initial investment of $10,000 into a low volatility (MM) or short duration bond fund. Suppose he chooses three equity UTs to invest $200 each UT/month, the $600 will be deducted monthly by selling away units equivalent to $600 from the $10,000 MM or short duration bond UT instead of $600 monthly from the bank account.

This is a good strategy as MM and short duration bond UTs on average has returned 1.2% to 3.5% annualised over the last 10 years and far exceeded the 0.1% p.a interest Singapore bank account gives. Therefore Jack will be better off deducting the monthly investments into the three equity UTs by auto selling units of the MM or short duration bond UT than deducting via giro from the bank account.

6.3 Herd Mentality Investing

Throughout history, there is always a group of investors who will follow the herd or follow their friends when they invest. For UTs they like to look at the top volume in equity and bonds UT for the past week and the past month. They also like to look at the monthly factsheets of the UTs to see if the fund sizes of the UTs they have been tracking have increased or decreased and by how much. Often times, it is not easy to find out how much exactly of the change in fund size is attributed to fresh investments inflow/outflow or the change in fund size was due to appreciation of the value in holdings and companies within the UT.

Such investors will also follow the recommendations of famous analysts on TV, radio or brokerage firms after they have upgraded the outlook for certain sector or initiated buy coverage, often times without doing much independent research on the suitability of the UT for themselves. There is also another group of investors who chase after the flavour of the month/quarter/year, without realising that many of these UTs have already risen in their NAV.

Professor Craig Israelsen in his article in *Financial Journal* for Nov 2013 studied the outcome if investors had perfectly selected the best investment asset class in the US between 1 Jan 1998 to 31 Dec 2012 (out of the 12 asset classes which includes eight equity classes of US Stocks (different caps), Non-US stocks, Real Estate Investment Trusts (REITs), Resources, Commodities, and four bonds and money market classes). He found out that if an investor with perfect knowledge and prediction had switched his/her entire holdings on Jan 1 to the best performing asset class for the year for consecutive 15 years then he/she would have achieved an incredible annualised return of 32.25%!

On the other hand, if an investor constantly 'rebalances' and switched his/her investments on Jan 1 to the best performing asset class in the previous year, he/she will only be rewarded with annualised returns of 2.71% throughout the 15-year period. The first investor with 32.25% annualised return also experienced lower variation in his returns compared to the investor chasing after the previous year's hot pick and asset class. Sadly, many investors are still coveting the best performing asset class of last year, although data and historical performance have shown that it is unwise and foolish. Prof Israelsen went on to highlight that it is near impossible for anyone to pick the best performing asset class/sector accurately for 15 consecutive years.

Forget the perfect portfolio and perfect timing of *When* to buy *What* as it is like expecting humans to walk on water. However, I believe every investor can have an achievable model portfolio by following these two steps: a) incremental disciplined regular savings to save and invest more when our income increases or discretionary income increases due to reduction in expenses, and b) a yearly review and rebalancing since asset class performance rotates given economy goes through cycles and shifts and also technology advances.

Some investors who follow the herd even took the initiative to check out what companies famous investors are buying and follow their lead. For example, they search for Warren Buffett's stock purchases in 2014, or in a local context, Peter Lim's stock purchases in 2014. Do not get me wrong, this methods may have worked in the past and made the investor a fortune, but we have to be mindful of Berkshire Hathaway's portfolio, investment time horizon and financial muscles vs our own portfolio and muscles. Mr Buffett famously said that his favourite holding period is forever. How many investors have a holding period like his?

Key learning points

- It is almost impossible to know the when is the perfect time to invest; it is more rational to discuss different ways to invest in UT and finetune investment strategies according to the current and next phase of the economy.

- There are three main ways to invest: a) Lump sum, b) Monthly and c) Herd mentality investing.

- Investors can potentially benefit from Dollar Cost Averaging to smooth the volatility of the investments if they invest monthly, and reduce the disruption of emotions from investing and market timing. It will only work for investments on long term upward trend with fluctuations.

- For monthly investments, there are four further methods: DCA (constant investment amount monthly), UCA (constant number of units purchased monthly), DVA (adjust different monthly amount to invest based on the total value of investments and where it stands vs the goal) and lastly regular savings via deducting UT holdings of a MM or a short term bond UT.

7

Where to Buy Unit Trusts

In this chapter, I will first give an overview of Singapore's financial industry particular to the CIS (Collective investment scheme) segment, defined as any registered investment that pools investors together to invest in a product. Since UTs form a major part of the CIS segment, and knowledge is power, it will be useful to get a sense of the big picture and how the CIS segment has evolved in the last six years if you want to start investing in Singapore UTs. In the second half of the chapter, I will share what platforms investors can purchase UTs from.

7.1 Overview of the CIS segment in Singapore

Singapore's CIS total Asset under Management (AUM) had grown leaps and bounds over the last two decades from S$1.2 billion[15] at the end of 1994 to over S$38.3 billion[16] at end of 2013. This is a growth of over 32 times!

The first chart below shows the AUM of the CIS industry in Singapore since 2007 to 2013. The AUM for CIS at the end of 2013 was still not at 2007 levels (before the global financial crisis) even though the total AUM (both discretionary and under advisory) by Singapore-based financial institutions (banks, finance and treasury centres, capital markets services licensees, financial advisers, insurance companies, etc.) at the end of 2013

($1,818 billion) had already exceeded 2007 ($1,173 billion) in the second chart.

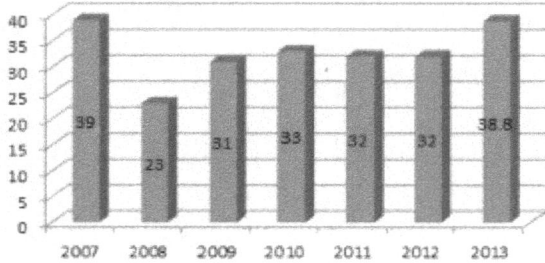

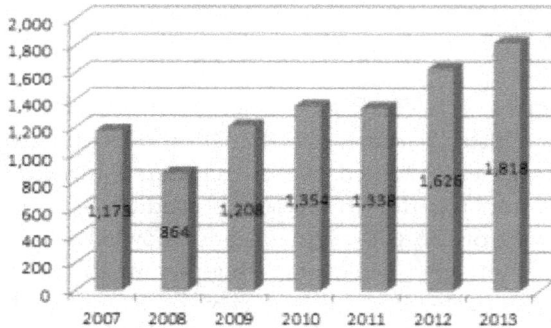

The next chart shows the percentage of total AUM managed by financial institutions in Singapore segregated by asset classes annually. We can see that in 2007 equities constituted about 57% of the total due to the prices of stocks hitting record highs and herds of investors rushing in to buy. By Q4 of 2007, equity markets were already declining and the entire 2008 was largely a bearish year for worldwide equities. This resulted in the percentage of equities that made up total AUM managed by Singapore financial institutions plunging from 57% to 43% as there was a flight to safety by fund managers and investors rebalancing their portfolios and shifting their investments into bonds (increase from 12% to 17%) and cash/MM (increase from 12% to 20%).

Short duration high grade bonds and the cash/MM asset class held their values very well for the entire 2008, so even if we exclude the inflow into these asset classes, by the end of 2008 their values would have constituted a bigger percentage of the overall AUM. Equities subsequently increased back to 51% in 2009 when investors returned after they felt markets had bottomed out in 2008.

We saw a similar situation from 2010 to 2011 because of the fears and talks about double dip recession unfolding in the Eurozone Sovereign debt defaults: equities dropped from 51% to 41%, and bonds and cash/MM increased from 16% to 20% and from 12% to 15% respectively. These fears subsided in September 2012 when the European Central Bank announced free unlimited support for countries that needed the bailout if they agreed to certain conditions like government spending cuts and raising tax rates, etc.

Year	Equities	Bonds	CIS	Cash/MM	Alternatives
2007	57%	12%	7%	12%	12%
2008	43%	17%	5%	20%	15%
2009	51%	16%	8%	14%	11%
2010	51%	16%	8%	12%	13%
2011	41%	20%	10%	15%	13%
2012	44%	23%	9%	12%	12%
2013	47%	23%	9%	8%	14%

The pie charts show the geographical spread of Singapore's CIS industry from 2007 to 2013. "Others" refers to the Middle East, Africa and Latin America regions. The bulk of Singapore's CIS is still invested in Asia Pacific all these years post the 2008 global financial crisis. The Eurozone crisis, which started in late 2009, resulted in Europe allocation of Singapore's CIS being heavily sold down from 18% in 2008 to 13% in 2009 to only 5% in 2010 because of the austerity measures implemented after the member states got the emergency bailout. We also observed that CIS investments in the US region dropped from 8% in Dec 2012 to 3% in Dec 2013 even though the Dow Jones and S&P 500 indices had hit record highs in late 2013. This could be due to many fund managers and investors taking profit and rebalancing their investments to add weight into Asia Pacific region throughout the year in 2013.

Pie charts: Singapore Investment of funds by asset class

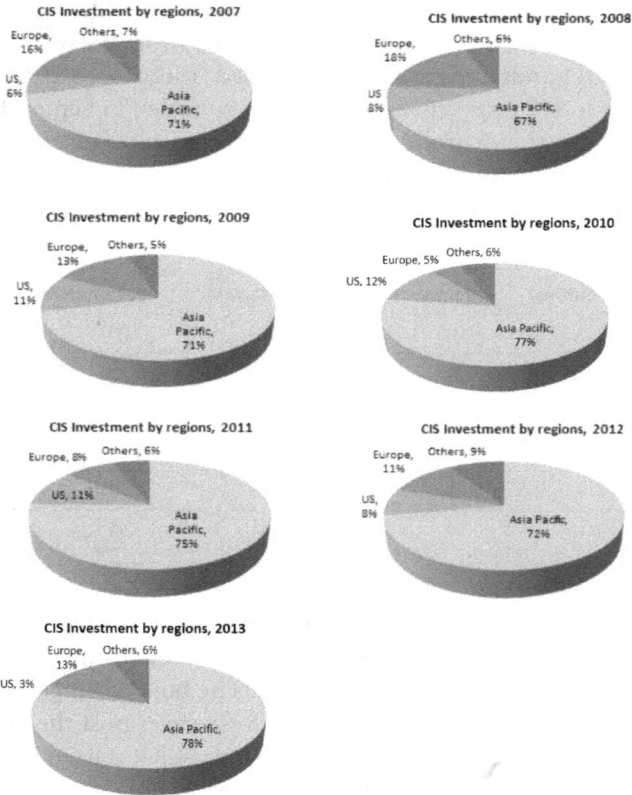

CIS Investment by regions, 2007
Europe, 16%   Others, 7%
US, 6%
Asia Pacific, 71%

CIS Investment by regions, 2008
Europe, 18%   Others, 6%
US 8%
Asia Pacific, 67%

CIS Investment by regions, 2009
Europe, 13%   Others, 5%
US, 11%
Asia Pacific, 71%

CIS Investment by regions, 2010
Europe, 5%   Others, 6%
US, 12%
Asia Pacific, 77%

CIS Investment by regions, 2011
Europe, 8%   Others, 6%
US, 11%
Asia Pacific, 75%

CIS Investment by regions, 2012
Europe, 11%   Others, 9%
US, 8%
Asia Pacific, 72%

CIS Investment by regions, 2013
Europe, 13%   Others, 6%
US, 3%
Asia Pacific, 78%

(Source: 2008–13 Singapore Asset Management Industry survey, Monetary Authority of Singapore)

7.2 Online distribution channel

After understanding Singapore's UT landscape better, the following section discusses platforms for buying UT. Investors can go online to buy UT, which usually has lower upfront fees, sometimes even reaching 0% with ongoing promotions. Of course, there will be no one to provide recommendations and the investor must understand his/her unique risk profile and decide which UT is suitable for him/herself. Investors will also be responsible for monitoring his/her UTs as monthly statements may be inadequate or come too late, especially in periods of crisis. One benefit of this, however, is convenience. You can buy/sell UT without going through a middle man at any time of the day and in any part of the world as long as you have a laptop and internet connection.

Currently there are three major players in the online UT distribution market in Singapore. They are a) Fundsupermart (owned by iFAST), b) Dollardex (owned by Aviva) and c) POEMS (owned by Phillip Securities Pte Ltd). The three platforms also provide free educational seminars for investors to attend, free research articles to read, as well as the peace of mind and assurance they are licensed by MAS and owned by a bigger parent company. At the time of writing in June 2014, here are the individual platforms' unique selling points.

I personally recommend FSM. Not only do they have a better user interface, it is also easier to use the account and software. Moreover, it offers more funds and more fund houses to choose from, the lowest upfront fee for bonds and equities UT, and the lowest switching fees. Although they are the only one charging a platform fee, their online and offline support, as well as the mailing out of fund notices and dividends cheques is always timely and accurate.

For a start, investors can choose to open an account with FSM and invest the initial sum with them as they have the most number of UTs available, lowest initial sales charge. Moreover, with a standard 7% Goods and Services Tax (GST) on the initial sales charge, FSM's total upfront charges will even be lower than Dollardex and POEMS especially if investment amount is $200,000 or more. If after a couple of months, they are dissatisfied for whatever reason, they may switch over to POEMS or Dollardex easily by opening a new account, submitting the UT statement from FSM and following the simple transfer instructions online. Alternatively, investors can open three accounts simultaneously, since all three platforms offer free account opening, and choose which one they like the most. Take note, however, that fees can be revised by all three platforms anytime; hence it is good to at least have active accounts with two platforms so the investor can decide which platform and interface he/she prefers.

Cost	Fundsupermart (FSM)	Dollardex	POEMS
Initial Upfront Fees (MM)	0%	0%	0%
Initial Upfront Fees (Bonds UT)	0% for selected bonds, otherwise 0.2% for investors with <$100k from 1 Sept 2014	0% for selected bonds, otherwise between 0.5% to 1.5%	0% for selected bonds with CPF-IA, otherwise 0.75%
Initial Upfront Fees (All other categories of UT)	0.5%, min of $10 per transaction. Can be only $10 if >$200,000 with FSM from 1 Sept 2014	Between 0.75% to 1.5%. Different client categories[17] enjoy discounts	0.75% Cash and SRS
GST on initial upfront fees	Yes	Yes	Yes
Switching fees	0 for same tier. 0.2% to 0.5% depends on category/tier of switched fund	0 for same tier. Calculated based on tier of UTs to be switched. Can be 0.5% to 1.5%	0.5% for same/different fund house or same/different group. 0.75% if switch out MM
Platform fees	0% for all CPF OA and SA. Cash/SRS, 0.2%p.a for fixed income and 0.5%p.a for other categories[18]	No platform fees	No platform fees
Number of UTs available	>600	>400	>400

7.3 Representative-assisted channel

Just like most people prefer to speak to an operator instead of an automated system when making a service or complaint call, I believe most investors prefer to interact with a representative of a financial adviser firm. This is even more so if this service bears the same costs and fees as investing online.

Investors who prefer a representative assisted channel may feel that every penny is well spent as they have either no expertise or no time to research and pick UTs for themselves or to monitor their investments. Some investors may have had bad experiences when they invested themselves. Others value the relationship they have built with the representative, who may also manage their family's insurance and other investments.

In Singapore, the three main channels that investors can buy UT via a representative are financial advisory (FA) firms, banks and insurance companies. Each has its own merits as well as shortfalls. Some FA firms in Singapore are Finexis, PIAS, etc and they use iFAST and Navigator (owned by Aviva) platforms. Banks and insurance companies also have their distribution channels, branches and online systems to service their clients.

For the banks not using the iFAST platform, there is likely no free switching of the UTs. If the switch is between two UTs belonging to the same fund house, the fee will be lower. If the switch is to another UT of a different fund house, the transaction will be treated like a fresh investment with another round of upfront fees. The investor at this point should also negotiate with the banks to lower the upfront fees for a second time, especially if they lost money on their first UT investment or barely made enough to cover another 3% to 4% of upfront fees.

For clients with a wrap account, the FAR can offer more objective advice on UT switching, rebalancing and management without being seen as churning the clients UT for another round of sales charge. One advantage of the wrap account is that the FAR can advice a switch when he/she feels there are better performing UTs of the same theme from another fund house compared to the existing UT the client is currently invested in. If it was a non wrap account, clients have to pay yet another round of sales charge even for a switch of similar theme UTs managed by different fund house. Personally, I favour wrap accounts since a) top UT fund managers can be headhunted by rival fund houses, b) top performing investment themes and geographical sectors rotate every few years, and c) the client's risk appetite and objectives may shift due to changing life stages, job situations and investment priorities.

Cost	Financial Advisory (FA)	Banks	Insurance Company
Initial Upfront Fee CPF OA/SA	Up to 2.8%, with 7% GST on upfront fees.	Up to 3%	Up to 3%
Initial Upfront Fee Cash/SRS	Up to 5%.	Up to 5%.	Up to 5%.
GST on upfront fees	Yes	No	No
Switching Fees	There will be unlimited free switches with a wrap account. Wrap fees can be up to 2% p.a. of investment portfolio AUM for cash/SRS.	Switching comes with a fee. Some banks based on same fund house switch, fee will be lower, if not will be another round of upfront fees.	Free switching for investment-linked plans (ILPs) and non ILP UTs for some insurance company
Platform Fees	Up to 0.3% p.a. No platform fees for CPF OA/SA.	No.	No.
Number of UTs	>600	Range between 150 to 400 UTs	Range from <50 to 150

Insurance companies like to bundle UTs with insurance coverage; this is called an investment-linked plan (ILP). ILPs usually have Death and Total Permanent Disability (TPD) benefits and provide an additional 5% to as much as 10% (for some ILPs) on top of the investment amount as insurance. So throughout the investment, even when the value of the UT falls below 105% of the invested amount or premiums, the investor is assured of at least 105% of the original invested amount upon death or TPD. However, this coverage has insurance charges, which are debited from the unit holdings every three or six months. If the ILP made more than 5%, then there is no additional coverage against death and TPD and so there will not be any insurance charges in this case. ILPs also have free fund switching within their suite of funds but with a small selection of around 20 to 30 UTs. Investors wanting to separate their insurance from their investments can ask their insurance representatives to recommend non-ILP options. An example of a pure UT product by an insurance company is AIA's Asset Evolution funds, which does not contain insurance charges as of the point of writing.

Key learning points

- The bulk of Singapore UTs are invested in Asia Pacific region.

- There are two main avenues to buy UTs: online and representative assisted channels.

- The three big online platforms to buy UT are Fundsupermart, Dollardex and POEMS. Each has its pros and cons.

- The three main players for representative assisted channel are financial advisory firms, banks and insurance companies. Each also has its pros and cons.

- History has shown it is not wise to invest with a herd mentality, by chasing after yesteryear's investment theme with best returns, or following other famous investors purchases without doing independent analyses and research on the suitability of the investment for the investor.

Endnotes

15. Written for Public Mutual Berhad in April 2008 by Ms Eileen Lian.
16. Source: 2008–13 Singapore Asset Management Industry survey, Monetary Authority of Singapore
17. Dollardex has three categories of clients (Standard, AUM of lesser than $25,000 will pay up to 1.5% for sales charge for equity UT) (Private Client, AUM of $25,000 to $200,000 will pay up to 1.2% for equity UT)/ (Private Client+, AUM of >$200,000 will pay up to 0.75% for equity UT)
18. Fundsupermart's platform fees have a lower tier when the investor has more money invested with them. 0.5% per annum for first $50,000, 0.44% for $50,001 to $200,000, 0.36% on $200,001 to $500,000 and 0.2% for remaining amounts above $500,000.

How to Read the Fund Factsheet, Product Highlight Sheet and Prospectus

There are three important documents that all investors should read before investing. This is even if the person is a seasoned UT investor or has bought the same UT before. They are the a) Fund factsheet, b) Product highlight sheet and c) Prospectus. This chapter will highlight key sections to look at within these documents.

8.1 Fund factsheet

The fund factsheet is usually two to three pages long and is often the document used by FARs to present the UT to prospective investors. Although the layout differs between different fund houses, the content and sections should be pretty similar. Important sections of the factsheet are the:

- UT investment objectives and strategy (the UT's investment mandate)

- Key information (the start date of the UT; upfront, switching and management fees; fund size; minimum investment amounts; source of funds that investors can use to invest in this UT, as well as the benchmark/comparison for this UT)

- ISIN (International Securities Identification Number) code (every UT's unique ID number; investors can google the ISIN to retrieve more information and charts from different websites)

- (Occasionally) Fund manager's name

The factsheet will also contain a chart showing the performance of the UT since its inception. If it has more than ten years of history, then the chart will likely show only the last five years. For different time periods of its historical performance, investors can look at the annualised and cumulative performance over the last three months, one year, three years, five years and since inception periods. The investor can compare the performance of a competitor UT with similar investment objectives or the benchmark stated in the factsheet if these can be found, by comparing these only then will the figures in the performance table makes sense.

Next important section the investor ought to pay attention should be the top 10 holdings. These are the ten securities the UT has the largest exposure and weight, investors can even work out the approximate amount of each holding using the individual percentage to the total fund size. At this point, the investor should also consider his/her existing investments and note if he/she is overexposed to certain companies or sectors after investing in this UT.

Investors should also look at the geographical allocation (especially for global or regional equity/bond UT) and the sector allocation. For bonds and MM UT, the factsheet might also indicate the weighted average maturity duration of the bonds, number of bonds within the UT, and the weighted average credit rating or the percentage of the bonds within the fund that falls into each grade (AA, A, BBB, etc). After examining this information, the investor must ask:

- Is the weighted average maturity duration of the bonds in the bond UT (e.g., 3.27 years) acceptable?

- What will the global interest rates environment over the next 3.27 years be like?
- What are the chances the economy does poorly and these companies in the UT holdings default (do not pay interest on the bonds they borrowed from the UT) or go bankrupt?
- Is the percentage of bonds that are BBB or even CC rated in the UT acceptable?

If the investor decides against a certain UT, he/she should always select another UT or ask the FAR to recommend an alternative. Lastly, the investor should also read through the last section which is usually the disclaimers and risk disclosures before deciding to invest.

After reading the product factsheet, and if the investor likes the investment objective, top 10 holdings and geographical investments, and can accept the risks. If he/she is also confident of the future outlook and performance of the UT, then the next step will be to read its product highlight sheet.

8.2 Product highlight sheet

This is a document that complements the factsheet and prospectus. It is usually four to six pages long and written in as jargon-free English as possible for investors to understand the key features and risks of the UT. The first section will list the important parties of the UT—the fund manager, custodian and trustee— as well as the launch date, expense ratio, etc. Also look out for dealing frequency—which indicates whether the UT has daily dealing and allows for buy/sell every day or weekly dealing; over 95% of UTs sold in Singapore are daily dealing—and whether it is capital guaranteed (over 95% of UTs sold in Singapore are not capital guaranteed).

The next section will be the product suitability section. This indicates which group of investors are suitable for this UT, and shows the page of the prospectus that investors can cross reference at the right hand column to read on the investment objectives and focus of the UT.

The next three sections on key product features (the structure of the UT, which gives more information on where and what kind of securities the UT will invests in), investment strategy (how and what the fund manager intends to do to grow investor's monies), and parties involved (fund manager, trustee, and custodian; if there is a parent fund this UT feeds into, it will reflect the parent fund manager). The investor must feel comfortable with the key product features and the key parties of the UT, and understand and feel optimistic on the investment strategy of the fund managers.

The next section, "key risks" is very important. If the investor does not understand any part of this section, he/she needs to clarify with the FAR. If he/she still feels uncomfortable, then it is better to choose another UT. The key risks listed are similar for MM, bonds and equity UTs and include market risks (economic conditions, interest rates, currency, etc), credit risks (default of the borrowers and the parties that the UT lent out money to), and liquidity risks (the investor can only sell their investments on dealing days which are typically the business days).

Different UTs will have slightly different product specific risks, the common ones being political risks and derivatives risk (if the UT employs derivatives or hedging techniques to manage the portfolio). Some UTs that make dividend distributions may warn potential investors that these distributions could face a risk that dividends will be paid out from the UT's capital if total dividends and capital appreciation from the companies within the holdings are insufficient. If the UT is narrowly focused and invests in single country or single sector, its product highlight sheet has to stress this concentration risks to potential investors.

The next section after product specific risks is fees and charges. The UT has to disclose this to prevent investors from getting a shock after they invest. The typical sales charges for investing in UT using non-CPF funds (cash and SRS) is up to 5%, and for CPF monies is up to 3%. The fund house must disclose the realisation or 'exit' charges although over 95% of Singapore UTs do not have an 'exit' charge at the point of writing because they already collect an upfront sales charge. Other charges include management fees, trustee fees, and if it is a feeder fund, they will also disclose the charges paid to the parent fund, which is typically a percentage of the total assets under management of the fund.

The second last section is on sources where the investor can obtain the pricing of the UT as well as the exit procedure plus the risks and any costs involved if the investor wants to fully sell off the UT.

The final section of the product highlight sheet is the contact information. They usually have a Singapore representative office number and website listed. If investors have any queries, even if it is fund related enquiry, do approach FARs or the UT distributor before approaching the fund house. This is because the representative or distributor has their records and other investors may have posted similar questions to them before. If both the FAR and distributor do not have an answer, they will approach the fund house on behalf of the investor.

8.3 Fund house prospectus

This is the thickest document of the three, and can be around 300 pages especially if the fund house is managing many UTs, so investors need to know the important sections to focus on. If the investor is short of time, he can zoom in to the section of the particular UT that he is considering.

The important sections are the key parties of the fund house and their roles. The prospectus will also mention if the UT has other underlying funds as well as the name and the country of domicile of the underlying fund.

The prospectus provides much more detail than the fund factsheet and product highlight sheet on important details like the UT's investment objectives and approaches, fees and charges (commissions, etc.), and risks. This document is edited and vetted by lawyers, and is much more technical in describing the UT. It also addresses the operational aspects (buying, switching and selling of units in the trust), where to obtain latest prices of the UT, and the performance of the fund house UTs.

The last section of the prospectus will mention scenarios arising from conflict of interest for the managers, and what they will do about it, other *material information* of the funds (important for the investor to at least read and understand), disclaimers, and information on where to obtain their annual audited reports.

Key learning points

- The three important documents the prospective investor must read before investing in the UT are the fund factsheet, product highlight sheet and prospectus.

- Key sections of the fund factsheet are the UT investment objectives and strategy, key information, and the UT's ISIN (which can be used to retrieve information and performance charts from different websites). Investors should next look at the top 10 holdings/securities that the UT invests in, and do more research on these individual companies. Next, it is important to look at the geographical allocation of the UT, and ask yourself if you are comfortable with investing in these regions and countries.

- If the investor is considering bonds UT, he/she should also look at the average maturity duration of the bonds from the factsheet. Consider what is the likely global interest rates environment from now until the average maturity duration, the average credit quality of the bonds, the percentage of BB or BBB bonds as a percentage of the total UT fund size and lastly the likelihood of defaulting or bankruptcy.

- In the product highlight sheet document, investors have to look out for important parties of the UT, launch date, dealing frequency, and the expense ratio. The next section is the product suitability and list parties suitable for the UT. The next three sections add more information, on top of the factsheet, on key product features, investment strategy and parties involved. It is followed by the key risks of the UT. It is important that investors read though the key risks and raise questions, if any. This is followed by the fees and charges, which are equally important for investors to note. The last two sections talk about sources of information for investors to obtain the NAV and the exit procedure (risks and costs involved) when they fully sell the UT. Lastly, they provide the contact information of a local representative office.

- Even though the prospectus is very thick, it is recommended that investors still read the entire prospectus. If not, use the contents page to navigate to the key sections or to pages that the product highlight sheet cross references to the prospectus. Other key sections to read, not covered by the factsheet and product highlight sheet are the conflict of interest for the managers, other material information of the funds as well as disclaimers and where to obtain their annual audited reports.

9

Which Categories of Unit Trust to Buy

In this chapter, I will explain the different categories of UT in greater detail. I will also list their risk ratings from 0 (lowest risk) to 10 (highest risk) in a chart below, adapted from the risk ratings for the funds from the iFAST platform. I will select a couple of UTs of SGD fund currency from each category and will do further analysis on them with the help of financial ratios so that the comparison is more meaningful. Please note that the UTs selected in this chapter are not necessarily superior to other UTs in the market.

The financial ratios used in this chapter for comparing performance between similar UTs are:

- *Annualised Returns*: It is important to look for the annualized returns of the fund for as long a period possible, the best is since its inception or start date of the fund. With longer track records we can look at the UT's performance during different periods of the economic cycle.

- *Min-Max NAV vs Current NAV*: Again, try to get as long a period of reference as possible if there are available data. This parameter is more meaningful when comparing equity UTs or UTs that are more volatile.

- *Annual Expense Ratio (AER)*: Described above in section 2.7

- *3-year Annualised Volatility*: Volatility is the measure of variation of prices over a period of time. The lower the volatility, the lesser the variation or difference of the prices of the financial instrument. After the global financial crisis in 2008, more investors are seeking lower volatility financial instruments, as they do not wish to experience high price differences in their investment portfolio. We would often candidly refer to high volatility investments as roller coaster investments. For UTs with volatility less than 1, investors can sleep very well at night.

- *3-year Risk-Return Ratio*: Risk-Return Ratio (RRR) is a measure of the return in terms of its risk. The higher the RRR, the better is its performance usually. This is fully comparable between different funds, as long as it is for the same time period.

- *3-year Sharpe Ratio:* Sharpe ratio is a measure of an investment's performance by adjusting for its risk. The higher the Sharpe ratio, the better its performance.

RRR and Sharpe Ratio may seem very similar in their definitions. I purposely include both of them in my analysis to give greater depth of comparison. This is because if an investor is comparing five or six different UTs within the same category, and there is one UT that wins in both RRR and Sharpe ratio, it is likely that is the winning UT and a 'better' investment. However if one of the UT wins in RRR and the other UT wins in the Sharpe ratio, then the investor should calculate their percentage difference between the winner and the second and third place in both their RRR and Sharpe ratios. The winner will be the UT with the bigger percentage lead.

Highest Risk, Highest potential returns

```
      10 ┌─
           │
       9 ─  Thematic (8 to 10)    Sector (8 to 10)

Equity UT      Equities (7 to 10)
                 Global equities 7
       8 ─       Regional equities 8
                 Country equities 9

       7 ─  Alternatives (6 to 10)
                 Risk rating depends on strategy
                 used, UT objectives and holdings

       6 ─  Balanced (5 to 7)
Balanced UT
       5 ─

           High Yields (4 to 6)
             Global high yields 4
       4 ─   Emerging market and Asia bonds 5 – 6

       3 ─

Fixed Income UT
       2 ─  Bonds (1 to 4)
             SGD bonds 1 – 2
             Global bonds 2 – 4

       1 ─

       0 └  SGD Money Market (MM)/Cash (0)
```

Lowest Risk, Lowest potential returns

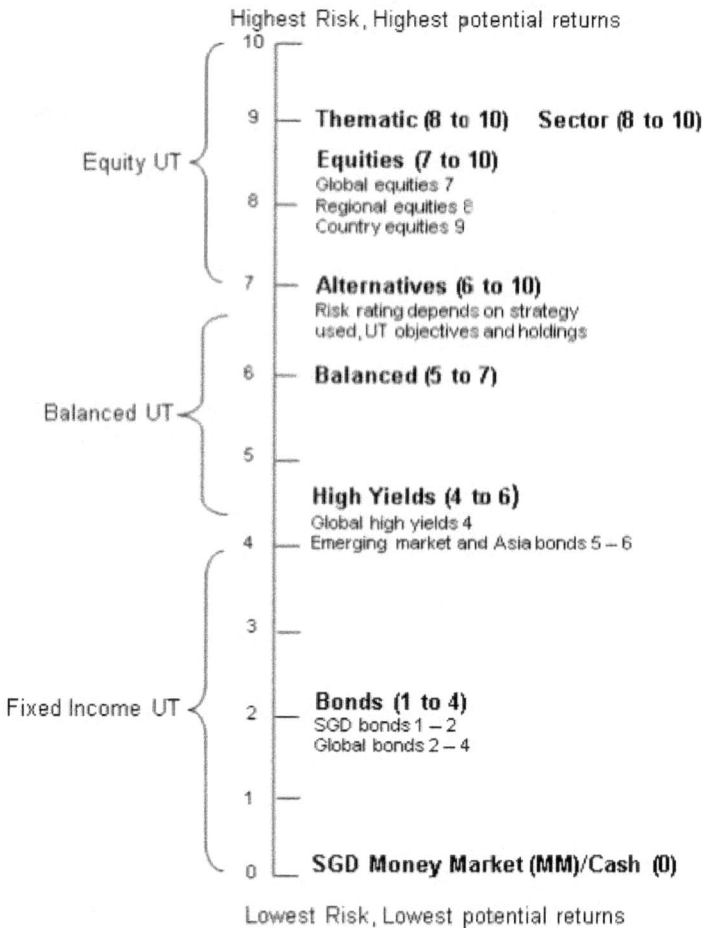

1. Money Market (MM): Safest category of UT. Holdings are made up of short duration high quality 'A' grade bonds. It is a safe haven category of UT for investors to switch into during periods of crisis and early days of recession in equity markets.
2. Short duration bonds: This is the second safest category of UT. Holdings are usually good quality MM or short-term bonds. This category of UT is very suitable for investors who are adverse to risk and volatility.

3. High-yield bonds: This category of UT is riskier than MM and short duration bonds, and it is possible to see declines of 20–30% in a year. Holdings are non-investment grade quality bonds, usually BBB and below. To compensate investors for the poorer credit quality of the bonds, they are rewarded with higher coupons and thus higher yields.

4. Balanced: This category of UT is a hybrid of equities and bonds. Even in times when the fund managers of the UT are very optimistic on equities, they still have to hold approx 30% in bonds and even in times when they are pessimistic on equities, they are also required by the UT mandate to hold at least 30% in equities. This category of UT is suitable for investors who want to leave the decision of the timing and percentage allocation of equity to bond entirely to the UT fund managers.

5. Alternatives: Risk ratings of Alternatives UTs vary, depending on the UT holdings and financial instruments used by the fund managers to achieve their objective. This category of UT seeks to give investors maximum returns while reducing the risk of loss and lowering the volatility of the UT.

6. Equities: Risk ratings of Equities UTs vary. As long as >90% of the total UT holdings are individual securities of companies, they are classified as equity UT. These include, single country, regional, global, thematic and sector UTs. Over any 15-year period, the average equities UT has a track record of outperforming bonds UTs, which in turn outperforms MM UTs.

7. Thematic: A higher risk type of UT, thematic UTs are UTs of a particular investment theme and most of them hold >90% equities. This category of UTs is suitable if investors have done their research and feel strongly on the future price appreciation of the equities within the thematic UT.

8. Sector: Another higher risk type of UT, sector UTs invest in equities of companies in a particular sector of the economy and hence is particularly vulnerable to risks that affect certain sector of the economy. Investors must do their research and due diligence before investing especially for sector and thematic UTs.

9.1 Money Market (MM) / Cash (risk rating 0)

Simple description: Most MM funds' investment objective is to preserve capital, maintain a high level of liquidity, and invest in high quality 'A' grade bonds for a short duration of no longer than two years. Most MM UTs will lend out and invest in SGD bonds. For example if they buy China bonds, the fund manager will use financial derivatives (financial contracts that derives its performance from the performance of another underlying asset) to hedge and minimise the currency conversion risks from RMB to SGD. They will also state whether financial derivatives are used.

Top Holdings: The top holdings in a MM fund are usually dominated by short duration bonds. How can one understand an individual bond as a security in a UT portfolio? You can look at this example:

- ABC X.XX% DDMMYYYY

- ABC: This is the borrower, also the company or entity that borrowed money from the MM UT.

- X.XX%: This is the repayment interest per annum that the borrower has to pay back together with the principal borrowed to the lender.

- DDMMYYYY: This is the date, month and year that the bond will mature/end, also the date that the borrower has to repay the principal.

Note that the grades of the bonds within the fund are equally important. Moody's Investor Services and Standard & Poor's are the two major bond rating agencies that make up 80% of the global market share. Just like restaurants and universities are rated and ranked, by rating every listed company with an internationally recognised standard based on their financial positions and other parameters, they help two main groups of people: the local and international investors and the banks wanting to lend them money. Some published research concludes that Moody's tends to give more conservative ratings than Standard & Poor's, especially in the industrials and utilities sector.

Moody's top rating in ascending order is Aaa, Aa, A, Baa, Ba, B, Caa, Ca and C (C being speculative). Moody's uses a numeral behind each rating to add a further grading: the smaller the numeral, the more creditworthy it is (e.g.,A1, Ca3, etc). Standard & Poor's top rating in ascending order is AAA, AA, A, BBB, BB, CCC, CC, C and D. They use a "+" or a "−" behind each rating to add further grading and no numerals (e.g., A+, BB-, etc.).

Most MM UT factsheets will show the percentage of the particular bond security out of the entire fund size. Hence investors will be able to get an accurate picture of how much (in millions) the UT has borrowed to the particular company/entity. Do not go ahead if you are not comfortable with, for example, over 30% of the entities in the top 10 holdings for fear they will go bankrupt or the operations of the business.

Performance ratios: I have chosen two popular MM UTs in Singapore for a deeper discussion.

- LionGlobal SGD Money Market (risk rating 0, started 1 Nov 1999)

- Phillip Money Market (risk rating 0, started 16 April 2001)

Comparables	LionGlobal SGD Money Market	Phillip Money Market
Annualised Returns	1.37%	1.15%
Min-Max NAV vs Current NAV	min $1.088, max $1.24, current $1.2375	min 1.0, max 1.1603, current: $1.16
AER	0.32%	0.5%
3-year Annualised Volatility	0.08	0.03
3-year Risk Return Ratio	6.38	16.67
3-year Sharpe Ratio	-23.75	-70.23

As of June 2014, the annualised returns for the last ten years are 1.37% for LionGlobal and 1.15% for Phillip, with their total returns at 14.58% and 12.15% respectively. When two UTs have different inception dates of more than 1.5 years apart, I personally prefer to use a common time frame like last five years or last ten years for a standardised comparison.

LionGlobal's current NAV (min 1.088, max 1.237) and Phillip's current NAV (min 1.0, max 1.16), is also their max NAV as at middle June 2014. LionGlobal has a lower AER of 0.32% vs Phillip with an AER of 0.5%. Thus we can then conclude that LionGlobal fund managers are more efficient in managing expenses for this money market UT vs Phillip. LionGlobal have a lower 3 year volatility of 0.08 while Phillip has 0.03 versus STI 13.12. The 3 year Risk-Return Ratio (RRR) of LionGlobal is 6.38 vs Phillip at 16.67. The 3 year Sharpe Ratio of LionGlobal is a -23.75 vs Phillip -70.23.

Phillip's RRR is higher than LionGlobal by 61% [(16.67–6.38)/16.67], however LionGlobal's Sharpe ratio is 195.7% [(-70.23%+-23.75)/23.75] better than Phillip. If investors can only choose one UT between these two, based on the last three years' data, I would urge investors to choose LionGlobal as they have an overwhelming lead in Sharpe Ratio.

My opinion: With reference to the chart below, that plots LionGlobal SGD Money Market vs Phillip Money Market vs the STI index we can see MM funds have very smooth linear lines, even during 2008 financial crisis. This is a good indication of MM funds behaviour in future crisis when equity markets suffer another major sell-off.

Therefore, MM UT is like a safe haven for investors to switch their higher risk equities and investments immediately when the VIX index shows a big spike for five consecutive months or more. The VIX index is also called the fear index or fear gauge and is a commonly used measure of investor's expectation of the volatility in the stock markets over the next 30-day period.

MM UT is also a good instrument for investors to return and re-invest back in the market while still uncertain of the bottoming of the market (*see* chapter 6 on ways of investing). Buy and Hold strategy for MM UT in the long term (over ten years) will definitely not make investors rich, given the annualised return is only approx 1.3% p.a. It will more likely make investors poorer in real terms as long term inflation rate is approx 3% in Singapore and thus the Sharpe ratio for both funds are very negative.

The chart also shows the Singapore Straits Times Index (STI), a basket of capitalization weighted stock market index comprising 30 of Singapore's biggest companies. It is also seen as a barometer of Singapore's economy. The STI from its highest recorded close of 3,875.77 (11 Oct 2007) to its lowest in the last ten years of 1,594.87 (27 Feb 2009). All it took was 16 months and 16 days to go from peak to trough.[19] The value was more than halved, a loss of 143%! Talk about sleepless nights especially if investors have used leverage to 'bet' on an earlier recovery before 27 Feb 2009.

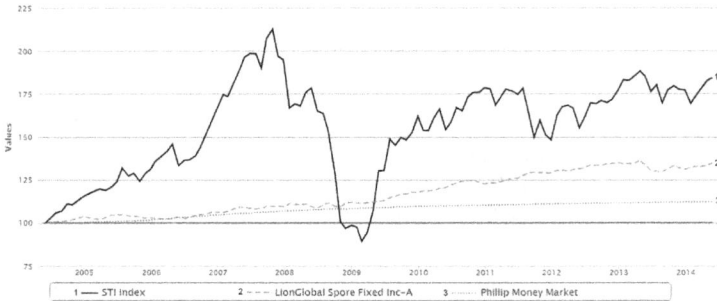

| 1 —— STI Index | 2 – – – LionGlobal Spore Fixed Inc-A | 3 ······ Phillip Money Market |

9.2 Bonds (risk rating 1 to 4)

Simple Description: There are a few kinds of bonds. In this section, I will touch on short duration bonds, and next section, I will cover high-yield bond.

The investment objectives of short duration bonds are pretty similar to MM funds, other than the fact that they their mandate allows them to lend out their funds for a longer duration than MM UT, not exceeding three or four years for some. More short duration bonds use financial derivatives to gear or leverage their positions compared to MM funds. Short duration bonds UT aim to preserve liquidity and capital and invest in a portfolio of good quality MM or short term bonds. Most of them benchmark their UT performance with Singapore's SIBOR (Singapore Interbank Offering rate) or SIBID (Singapore Interbank Bid rate). SIBOR is the daily interest rate that Singapore banks lend unsecured funds among one another. SIBID is less used these days.

Top Holdings: The top holdings of a bond UT are usually banking or financial firms. These big banks also enjoy good credit ratings like single A, and some even have better credit ratings than the governments of many developing nations.

Most Singapore bond UTs have over 40 holdings. From the top 10 holdings and the total percentage they constitute of the fund size, an investor may be able to estimate the UT's total holdings. This simple estimation can also be used for other categories of UT too.

Performance Ratios: I have chosen United SGD fund (risk rating 2, started in May 1998) and Nikko AM Shenton Short Term Bond Fund (risk rating 1, started in 29 Sept 2000) for a thorough analysis. Since these two UTs have inception dates of more than two years apart, we will look at the last ten years to compare their Annualised Returns and also Min-Max NAV. The last three factors take in their performance in the last three years.

Comparables	United SGD Fund	Nikko AM Shenton Short Term Bond
Annualised Returns	3.86%	2.43%
Min-Max NAV vs Current NAV	min $1.171, max $1.695	min $1.1, max $1.381
AER	0.63%	0.48%
3-year Annualised Volatility	1.55	0.83
3-year Risk Return Ratio	2.63	3.1
3-year Sharpe Ratio	0.98	0.06

The total return for United SGD over the last ten years is 45.94% and for Nikko is 27.09% respectively. Both their current NAV is also their max NAV as at middle June 2014.

Even though United's AER is more than 30% higher than Nikko, it seems for their superior performance in their Annualised and Total returns, especially in the last five years (chart below), it can rightfully justify their higher AER.

We can see that SGD short duration bond UT is also a low fluctuation and low volatility category of UT, although they have a higher volatility than MM UT.

Nikko's RRR is 17.8% better than United. However, United's Sharpe ratio is 1,533% better than Nikko, signifying that United has greatly outperformed Nikko by a large margin in the last three years. So investors who picked United instead of Nikko's short duration bond UT three years ago have been well rewarded.

My opinion: From the chart below, we can also see that short duration bond UT can also be very good safe haven during periods of fear and panic in the markets. Investors will have one more choice on top of MM funds to choose from.

Although they offer better annualised returns and have a positive Sharpe ratio compared to MM funds, these are still not at levels that adequately compensate investors for the sales charges. Hence the buy-and-hold strategy for this category of UT for the long term will not appeal to most savvy investors keen to beat inflation rate.

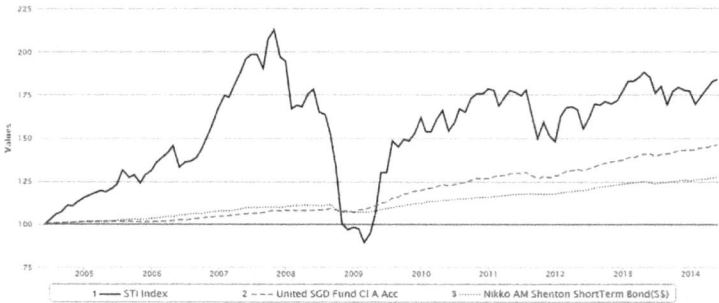

1 ——— STI Index   2 – – – United SGD Fund Cl A Acc   3 ········ Nikko AM Shenton ShortTerm Bond(S$)

9.3 High-yield bonds (risk rating 4 to 6)

Simple Description: The global equity markets have had its fair share of good and bad news, cancelling each other out from 2010 until the middle of 2014, a period many analysts and investors termed a "sideways market where there is neither a clear uptrend nor a downtrend." Hence in recent years, more investors are concerned with finding investments with better yields and payouts because of the sideways and volatile equity markets.

This investment climate and investor's appetite led to several fund houses launching high-yield bonds UTs to Singapore investors from 2010. Most of their investment objectives are simply to provide income and capital growth.

Top Holdings: Even though most high-yield bonds UTs have over 85% exposure in lending to institutions BBB and below, however their top 10 holdings is usually below 20% of the total fund size. What this means is the total UT fund size is spread across many institutions and holdings, so as to mitigate the impact to the UT's NAV if any single institution defaults or go bankrupt.

The holdings within high-yield bonds UTs usually have a longer duration when they issue out loans. They tend to lend out to corporate and government entities that usually have B, BB or BBB credit rating. High yields UT usually have fewer than 20% of their total fund size loaned out to A or better rated companies or borrowers as compared to the two short duration bonds in section 9.2, which has over 80% loaned out to A or better rated Companies.

Performance Ratios: I have chosen Eastspring Investments MIP M (risk rating 4, started 1 Feb 2005). This is one of the earliest high-yield bonds UTs in Singapore. I have also included Aviva Investors Global High Yield (risk rating 4, started 30 June 2010) and Fidelity Emerging Market Debt (risk rating 5, started 15 May 2006) as comparisons. As Aviva Investors Global High Yield has only four-plus years of inception history at the point of writing, I was only able to make comparisons over a period of three years for consistency.

Comparables (three years)	Eastspring Investments MIP M	Aviva Investors Global High Yield	Fidelity Emerging Market Debt
Annualised Returns (three yrs)	6.58%	8.42%	6.71%
Min-Max NAV vs Current NAV (three yrs)	$0.909, $1.077 vs $1.011	$9.738, $11.468 vs $11.301	$0.867, $1.028 vs $0.977
AER	1.4%	1.53%	1.66%
3-year Annualised Volatility	4.55	4.54	5.86
3-year Risk Return Ratio	1.45	1.85	1.15
3-year Sharpe Ratio	0.88	1.26	0.71

Even though high yields are classified as one sub category of the bonds family, the 3-years AER for high-yield bonds UTs are more similar to some equities UTs and other higher volatility

UTs than short duration bonds. The total returns in the last 3 years are as follow: Eastspring 21.08%, Aviva 27.41% and Fidelity 21.65% . From their min-max NAV vs current NAV (as of 20 Jun 2014), Eastspring seems to show more potential for upside as its current NAV is still approx 6.13% lower than its 3-year high vs Aviva's at 1.46% and Fidelity at 4.96%

Among the three funds, Aviva is the clear leader in both the RRR and Sharpe Ratio comparison. Therefore, it is quite obvious which high-yield bonds UT has performed the best in the last three years. Aviva Investors Global High Yield Bond fund is a select group of less than 5% of UT sold in Singapore to have 3-year RRR and Sharpe ratios of over 1 in the last three years as at middle June 2014.

My opinions: High-yield bond UTs are definitely more volatile and have higher AER than short duration bonds UTs. However investors have been well rewarded for taking higher risks the last three years as this class of bonds UTs also offer better RRR and Sharpe ratio.

Eastspring Investments MIP M and Fidelity Emerging Market Debt UT have been in the market for about nine years and eight years respectively. Over a ten-year period, these two funds were still able to deliver 9.31% and 6.37% respectively compared to STI's return of 6.2%. During the global financial crisis of 2008, the STI had a steep plunge of 143%. Even though high-yield bonds UTs were not spared, their drop was only 25% to 30%, less than one-fifth of the STI sell down.

Even when the high-yield bonds UTs NAV prices were dropping during the financial crisis, the Eastspring and Fidelity Fund Managers still continued to pay dividends of between 4% to 6% p.a. such that these cushioned the drop in the NAV.

As Singapore progresses into the second and third decade of the twenty-first century, we will see a bigger percentage of our population aged above 65 because of longer life expectancy, low birth rates, etc. Hence an instrument that can provide monthly dividends/income is definitely very welcome. As far as I know, there are no stocks in Singapore that pay monthly dividends.

The fact that dividend income from bonds is definitely more stable and predictable than dividends from equities was proven when Lehmann Brothers filed for bankruptcy in Sept 2008. For the next two years, fewer than 25% of the listed companies in Singapore paid out dividends, but the two high-yield bonds funds from Eastspring and Fidelity continued their monthly payout, which is very important for retirees who needed the regular income for their daily necessities regardless of the turmoil in global stock markets.

9.4 Balanced (risk rating 5 to 7)

Simple Description: This category of UT is a hybrid between bonds and equities, hence the name Balanced or Blended. The Fund managers will decide on the current market and the potential direction of the markets 12 to 18 months down the road and adjust their bonds and equities composition accordingly. Even when the Fund managers are very bullish on equities, it is still common to see them keep a min of at least 30% of their holdings in bonds to keep in line with their investment mandate. The same is true even when they become bearish on equities; they are still required to keep and hold at least 30% of their fund size in equities.

The common investment objectives of balanced UTs are to provide long-term capital appreciation by active management and diversification into a portfolio with equities, bonds, commodities, etc.

Top Holdings: Two of the three funds I selected for a deeper comparison below (DWS and Schroder) are Fund of Funds. If you examine their factsheet closely, you will realise the DWS fund actually invests in DWS lion bond (to make up at least 30%

of their fund size in bonds) as well as invest in DWS Global equity fund and DWS Singapore Equity. Schroder also invest in their own funds Schroder Global Bond, Schroder Singapore Trust, Schroder Japanese Equity, etc. So fund of funds is essentially a fund that invests and has holdings in other funds.

Performance Ratios: I selected three funds for a deeper discussion: DWS Premier Select Trust (risk rating 6, started 29 Nov 1993), First State Bridge (risk rating 6, started 2 June 2003) and Schroder Multi-Asset Revolution (risk rating 6, started 1 April 1998). I choose these three funds because they are popular balanced funds with over ten years of performance track records. All these three funds are also on the approved CPF SA fund list, meaning the UTs have met certain criteria and accept investors' CPF Special Account funds for investment.

Comparables	DWS Premier Select Trust	First State Bridge	Schroder Multi-Asset Revolution
Annualised Returns	4.49%	8.64%	3.5%
Min-Max NAV vs Current NAV	$0.967, $1.587 vs $1.584	$0.918, $1.548 vs $1.494	$0.858, $1.292 vs $1.257
AER	1.54%	1.43%	1.56%
3-year Annualised Volatility	6.85	5.91	6.24
3-year Risk Return Ratio	0.84	0.99	0.81
3-year Sharpe Ratio	0.49	0.57	0.43

Their total returns over the past ten years are, ignoring the upfront sales charge, DWS 55.59%, First State Bridge 75.64% and Schroder Multi-Asset 41.59%. Balanced UTs are considered slightly riskier than high-yield bonds UT with almost the same AER. Their RRR and Sharpe ratio are lower than high-yield bonds UTs in the past three years. Of the three funds, First State Bridge seems to have performed better, indicated by its RRR and Sharpe ratio and its annualised returns.

My opinion: Some investors asked how necessary balanced UTs are in their portfolio. It is possible to use 50% of their investment capital to buy a good equity fund and the remaining 50% to buy a good bond fund, which potentially results in a balance risk rating portfolio, instead of investing 100% in a balanced UT. If the investor chooses this option, he/she will have to monitor and do the switching between the equity and bond composition according to the market cycle.

Furthermore many balanced UTs are fund of funds, apparent from their top 10 holdings. Usually fund of funds may incur a second layer of management fees. The issue of *transparency* is important: for obvious reasons the balanced fund UT will only choose funds belonging to their own fund house in their portfolio. We can see this from the holdings of DWS Select Premier Trust and Schroder Multi-Asset Revolution. The investor will have to make a judgement on whether the Balanced UT fund manager is holding the best equity fund and best bond fund they can find, or if they are obliged to hold one from their own fund house.

One of the advantages that several balanced UT have over other categories of UT is they are CPF SA approved. They have arguably the highest risk rating 6, that an investor in Singapore can use their CPF SA to invest. Especially for First State Bridge, even with sales charge factored in, it is one of the few UT with annualized returns outperforming the guaranteed CPF SA interest rate, which at this time of writing is 4%. This is quite remarkable considering this included the period of the global financial crisis of 2008.

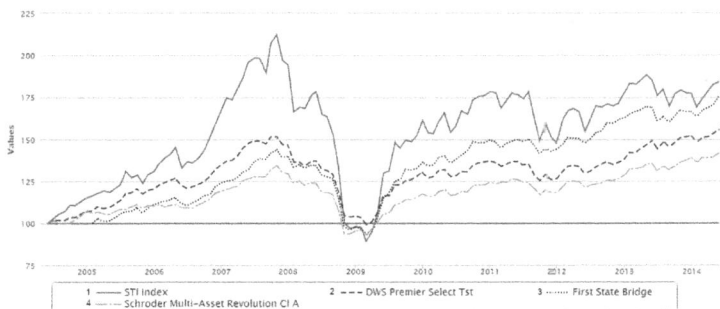

9.5 Alternatives (risk rating 6 to 10)

Simple Description: The fund objective of many Alternatives UTs is to give investors maximum total returns while trying to reduce the risk of loss and lower the volatility of the portfolio. Many fund managers also have the mandate to be flexible to adjust the fund portfolio according to and in anticipation of changing market conditions.

Many Alternatives UTs uses derivatives and other hedging strategies. Because of that, some Alternatives UTs do not have a reference or a benchmark to compare their performance to. As fund managers have the flexibility to manage their fund investing in different asset classes, they operate very similarly to hedge fund managers.

Top Holdings: Many of the alternatives UTs hold a mixed portfolio of equities, bonds (short duration, high yields, etc) and money market securities. They also use financial derivatives.

Their holdings are not limited by geography and sectors or industries of the economy. They are also not restricted to invest in non-SGD denominated investments and most of them have currency hedging strategies as seen from their fund name (Sgd-Hedged or Sgd-H).

Performance Ratios: The three funds I have selected for a deeper discussion are Allianz Global High Payout (risk rating 8, started 19 Dec 2005), Blackrock Global Allocation SGD-H (risk rating 6, started 30 July 2007) and UBS Dynamic Alpha SGD-Hedged (risk rating 6, started 19 April 2007). These three funds are chosen as they have a decent track record of more than five years, have been through the 2008 financial crisis, and share a number of similarities in their investment objectives.

Comparables (last five years)	Allianz Global High Payout Fund	Blackrock Global Allocation Fund	UBS Dynamic Alpha (SGD hedged)
Annualised Returns (last five years)	7.15%	8.04%	3.5%
Min-Max NAV vs Current NAV (last five years)	$0.466, $0.628 vs $0.541	$8.13, $12.23 vs $12.23	$76.79, $105.7 vs $104.85
AER	1.9%	1.77%	1.98%
3-year Annualised Volatility	10.58	8.32	5.47
3-year Risk Return Ratio	0.69	0.69	1.15
3-year Sharpe Ratio	0.48	0.41	0.69

Alternatives usually have higher AERs because of the derivatives, hedging costs, higher buying and selling activity volume and higher management fees charged, since alternatives requires higher degrees of management expertise. Although the three funds are classified as Alternatives, their volatility can have big disparities due to every individual manager's flexibility to manage the investments. Their total returns over last five years are Allianz 38.62%, Blackrock 44.26% and UBS 31.93%. UBS's annualised return has lagged behind even though their 3-year RRR and Sharpe Ratio is better because from June 2010 to June 2012 they have perform poorly. Their 3-year annualised volatility is also the lowest among the three funds, hence making their 3-year RRR look better.

My opinions: Alternatives are a newer class of UT funds as compared to bonds UT and equities UT. It is hard to predict the future performance of the alternatives UTs based on its past performance as fund managers have a lot of discretion and flexibility to change their holdings when they take certain views on the markets. It could take just a few good calls to turnaround a poorly performing UT and produce good double digit returns in just six months.

Certain alternatives UTs like the Blackrock Global Allocation Fund can have no minimum and no maximum equity, which means it is possible for the manager to avoid equity totally especially during middle 2007 to end of Q1 2009 when equity markets slid. So it would have been possible for the perfect fund manager of this UT to sell 100% of equities in mid-2007 when equity markets peak and to re-enter equities in Q1 of 2009 when it bottomed. Of course, this is easier said than done.

There are also alternatives UTs in the market like the Allianz Global High Payout that pay out attractive dividends. It pays approx 7% to 8% p.a. twice a year, which can be good income for retiree investors. Investors need to watch the NAV of such types of UT that pay out good income. This UT was launched in Dec 2005 at NAV $1 per unit; as of middle June 2014, the NAV has dropped to $0.541 per unit. For an investor who had invested in the UT from Dec 2005 to June 2014, even with the payout of 7% to 8% p.a, the absolute return since inception with the sales charge is still -0.62% p.a.

I would advise investors who are considering adding alternatives UTs to their portfolio to read the factsheet and the prospectus more thoroughly than other categories of UTs. It is important to understand the strategies the fund managers are using to maximise returns, also think about what kind of risks the fund might possibly have and if you can accept them. The investor also has to constantly look at the UT's AER and fund size because some alternatives and hedge funds UTs encountered heavy sell-off when there were major crises or rumours (whether true or unproven).

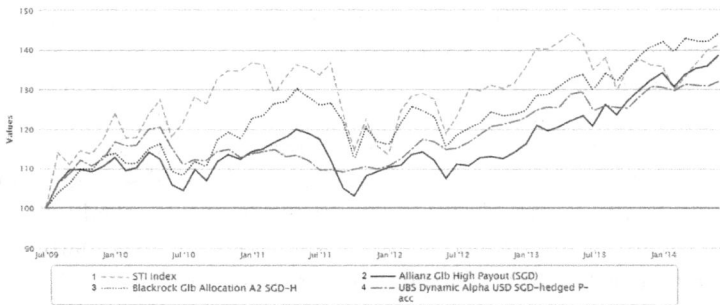

9.6 Equities UT (risk rating 7 to 10)

Simple Description: Equities UT is a broad category. Any UT with over 90% securities of companies in their holdings is considered a equity UT. Hence UTs that are not MM, bonds, balanced or alternatives are generally classified as equity UT. It includes index UTs mentioned earlier in section 1.2, thematic and sector UTs covered in the two subsections below, equity UTs that invest in single country securities, UT specializing in regional UTs, and UTs investing in global equities.

For this section, I will choose single country equity UT – Singapore. The investment objectives of single country equity UT is to provide investors with medium- to long- term capital growth by investing in listed companies in that country's stock exchange. The benchmark is often the country's principal stock index, STI in this case.

Top Holdings: As Singapore is poised to be a financial hub and services-oriented first-world city, the top holdings are more often than not dominated by securities of financials (DBS, UOB and OCBC). The next industry by holdings size is usually the industrials sector (Keppel Corp, Sembcorp, etc.)

Performance Ratios: The three funds I have selected for a deeper discussion are Aberdeen Singapore Equity (risk rating 8, started 5 Dec 1997), First State Singapore Growth (risk rating 9, started 25 Jul 1969) and Schroder Singapore Trust (risk rating 8, startd 1 Feb 1993). These three funds are chosen because all of them have a very long and good track record. First State Singapore Growth is not a 100% pure Singapore equity UT but has about 40% in Malaysia equities in their holdings. I included First State Singapore growth to give more depth in the discussion later.

Comparables (last ten years)	Aberdeen Singapore Equity	First State Singapore Growth	Schroder Singapore Trust
Annualised Returns (last ten years)	10.1%	11.97%	9.87%
Min-Max NAV vs Current NAV (last ten years)	($1.885, $5.178) vs $5.007	($1.041, $3.391) vs $3.348	($0.738, $1.916) vs $1.555
AER	1.67%	1.92%	1.32%
3-year Annualised Volatility	13.01	10.08	13.56
3-year Risk Return Ratio	0.56	1.37	0.47
3-year Sharpe Ratio	0.41	1.09	0.35

Their total returns for the last ten years are Aberdeen 163.22%, First State 213.7% and Schroder 107.95%. Many investors are shocked that the difference in Schroder Singapore Trust and Aberdeen Singapore Equity's returns is more than 60% over ten years. This is another reason many people may have negative comments or bad experiences with UTs. Even UTs with similar investment objectives and geographical regions can deliver stunningly different outcomes and results over time due to the fund managers of different fund houses buying and selling different quantities and securities and at different prices daily over a period of more than five years. Also, by engaging a competent representative, s/he can compare UTs across more fund houses and pick out UTs with better track records. Of course the more funds and bigger range of UT pool that the representative gets to shortlist from, the better his effectiveness to aid investors.

Although First State has the highest AER, investors are well rewarded by its remarkable annualised and total returns and also both the 3-years RRR and the Sharpe Ratio as compared to Schroder and Aberdeen. Remember earlier we discussed UTs with both the 3-year RRR and 3-year Sharpe ratio >1, the First State Singapore Growth is another UT in that pedigree which had delivered exceptional returns given the risk and volatility in the last three years.

First State Singapore Growth's NAV had risen 3.21 times in the last ten years to June 2014. By adding about 35–40% of Malaysia's big Companies in the portfolio, they are able to achieve lower 3-year annualised volatility compared to the two Singapore-only equity UTs.

My opinion: I believe every investor should have equities UTs in their portfolio, especially those from a single country or region that the investor is very familiar with in terms of the country's economic policies, political news, social trends, demographics and also business model of the top 10 holdings. He or she must also feel optimistic and bullish of the equities within the geographical region to invest there.

If the returns from bonds are slightly higher than Singapore's inflation rate of 3.5%, then holding only a portfolio of bonds and money market funds and expecting to save for retirement is next to impossible. Hence to build a winning portfolio, you will need some equity UTs, together with the right time to enter the market and the right amount of time staying invested.

To show investors the amazing effects of compounding returns and the wonders that UTs can bring to everyone's portfolio, I often use the First State Singapore Growth fund, which has delivered a return of 8.8% annualised (with initial charges and all management charges factored in) since it started in 25 July 1969. With the 'Rule of 72' which uses 72 as a number to divide by the annualised return (8.8%) to calculate the time it takes for investors to double their money, we get 8.18 years. So on average every 8.18 years, the investors in this fund would have doubled their money. With this fund being in the market for close to 45 years, investors would have doubled their monies

5.5 times! An investor who bought this fund and used a buy-and-hold strategy with $10,000 in July 1969 would have received quite a bit ($10,000 x 2 x 2 x 2 x 2 x 2.5 = approximately $400,000) in June 2014. The costs of a 3-room HDB[20] flat in Toa Payoh was about $7,500 in 1969. In mid-2014, a 3-room HDB flat in Toa Payoh costs approx $320,000 to S340,000. Therefore the price appreciation of First State Singapore Growth UT can be compared to the housing price increase of Singapore over the last 45 years.

Other investors often complain that equity UTs are more expensive and it is cheaper to buy exchange traded funds (ETFs). It is true since ETFs that track the STI index will have lower costs since they are passively managed. However, is this a case of being penny wise, pound foolish? Over the last ten years, including the global financial crisis in 2008, it is very obvious that the actively managed Singapore equities UT have outperformed ETFs tracking the STI index. Saving on the costs may not be worth it if you end up missing out on the far higher returns generated by paying a bit more to engage competent UT professionals.

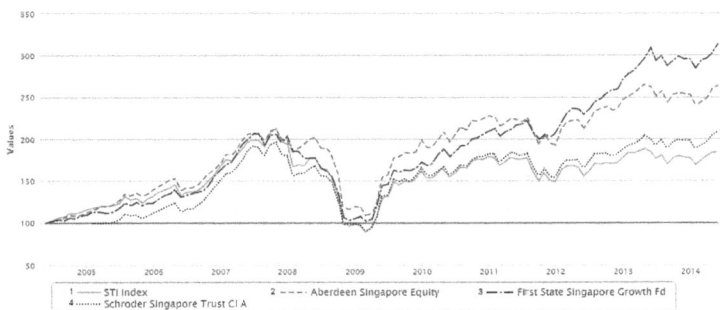

9.7 Thematic (risk rating 8 to 10)

Simple Description: Thematic UTs are investment themes or causes that investors feel attached to or strongly feel will increase in value.

Every thematic UT has its own unique investment objective. Amundi Global Luxury and Lifestyle UT invests in companies that produces luxury goods and services. The HSBC Global

Climate Change invests in companies that are involved in activities related to climate change. The First State Innovation Fund invests in companies that the fund manager believes to be innovative in its business practices (innovative capital structure, innovative use of technology, innovative employee incentives, etc.).

Other thematic UTs investors can buy into are:

- IPO (for investors who wants to invest in securities that are offered primarily in IPOs, post IPOs and debt securities that bear interests.)

- Islamic Theme (for investors who only want to invest in Shariah compliant equity and Shariah compliant fixed income called Sukuk. It is common to see Islamic theme UTs that hold little financials as the business of lending for interest is not seen as Shariah compliant. Businesses related to gambling or alcohol will not be considered by the fund managers of such UTs.)

- Internet Theme (for investors who want to invest in companies that are well positioned in the e-commerce trade.)

Top Holdings: The Global Luxury & Lifestyle fund is heavily concentrated on the consumer discretionary sector as these are luxury goods and services providers and not companies producing consumer staples or basics/essentials. The top few holdings are Daimler AG (producers of Mercedes), CIE Financial Richemont (They own brands like Cartier, Mont Blanc, IWC, etc.) The HSBC Global Climate Change's major holdings are in financials, oil and gas and consumer services companies. The First State Asia Innovation Fund has major holdings in consumer staples (Amorepacific Corp), financials (Cheung Kong Holdings) and industrials (Hutchison Whampoa).

Performance Ratios: The three funds I have selected for a deeper discussion are Amundi Global Luxury and Lifestyle SGD (risk rating 9, started 1 March 2007), HSBC Global Climate Change SGD (risk rating 9, started 9 Nov 2007) and First State Asia Innovation (risk rating 10, started 18 Oct 1999). As these funds have different individual themes, it may not serve much purpose to compare their performances.

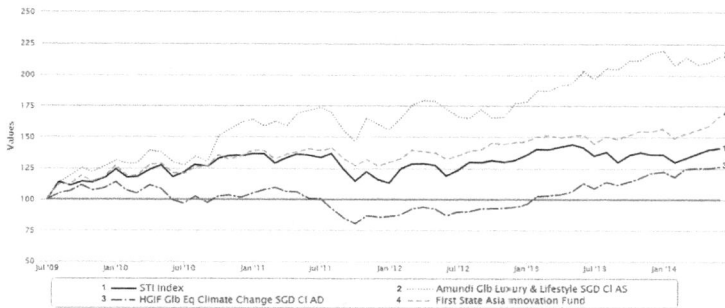

| | 1 —— STI Index | 2 ···· Amundi Glb Luxury & Lifestyle SGD CI AS |
| | 3 —·— HGIF Glb Eq Climate Change SGD CI AD | 4 — — First State Asia Innovation Fund |

Comparables (last five years)	Amundi Global Luxury & Lifestyle SGD	HSBC Global Climate Change SGD	First State Asia Innovation Fund
Annualised Returns (last five years)	16.54%	5.2%	11.15%
Min-Max NAV vs Current NAV (last five years)	$0.607, $1.377) vs $1.339	($6.06, $9.827) vs $9.8	($0.51, $0.89) vs $0.879
AER	2.18%	1.86%	2.1%
3-year Annualised Volatility	16.44	13.46	10.74
3-year Risk Return Ratio	0.6	0.7	0.68
3-year Sharpe Ratio	0.51	0.56	0.48

My opinion: Their total returns over the last five years are Amundi Global Luxury & Lifestyle 115.2%, HSBC Global Climate Change 26.31% and First State Asia Innovation fund 67.1%. Many thematic UTs do not have very good track records. Most of them have delivered less than 4% annualised since their inception. Unless the investor really feels for a certain investment theme, I advise investors to consider investing in other categories of UT to grow their investment nest egg.

9.8 Sector (risk rating 8 to 10)

Simple Description: Sector UTs invest in a particular sector or industry of the economy. Sector UTs and thematic UTs share the highest risk category of UTs.

The UT name provides very strong clues on what and which

sector the UT invests in. If the investor is familiar and feels optimistic on the growth of certain geographical regions, especially on certain sectors for fast paced growth, then he or she can invest in specific sector UT for faster upside gains.

Other sectors of Singapore UT that investors can directly buy into are:

- Consumer sector: if they feel strongly in the China-fuelled consumption theme.

- Finance sector: if investors are bullish on the prospect of banks and insurance companies due to rising interest rates, rising population, etc.

- Global Agriculture: if investors feel population growth and climate change will result in boom for companies in the agriculture sector.

- Gold and precious metals: if they feel share price of companies that mine the yellow metal and other precious metal prices will further appreciate.

- Healthcare: if investors think the ageing population and shifting demographics will create more demand for medical drugs and healthcare providers, etc.

- Infrastructure: if investors are optimistic on the securities of listed companies constructing expressways, railroads, power stations, etc. Particularly good in developing economies or when governments want to spend more on public goods.

- Property: if investors are optimistic on the shares of property developers and real estate investment trusts.

- Resources: if investors feel that energy and companies that mine precious resources will appreciate in future.

- Telecommunications: if investors are confident on the outlook of communications providers companies.

- Utilities: if investors feel that utilities companies will do well.

Top Holdings: The holdings of sector UT are usually the big name companies in that particular sector. They would be the market leaders and household names for most people. If the investor has not heard of the top 3 holdings but still would like to invest in that sector, do more research and read up more on the companies before investing.

Performance Ratios: The three funds I have selected for a deeper discussion are First State Global Resources (risk rating 10, started 25 Jul 2005), Henderson Global Technology (risk rating 10, started 13 Oct 1997) and United Global Healthcare (risk rating 10, started 12 Jul 2000). These three funds are intentionally chosen from different sectors of the economy. This is not to compare amongst them as they are from different sectors, but to illustrate the attractiveness of adding the right sector UT to the investor's overall portfolio, for investors with bigger risk appetite.

Comparables (last ten years)	First State Global Resources	Henderson Global Technology	United Global Healthcare
Annualised Returns (last ten years)	1.33%	5.29%	7.96%
Min-Max NAV vs Current NAV (last ten years)	($0.621, $2.003) vs $1.129	($0.84, $2.01) vs $2.0	($1.198, $3.171) vs $3.124
AER	1.66%	1.92%	2.16%
3-year Annualised Volatility	21.14	16.16	15.08
3-year Risk Return Ratio	-0.43	0.86	1.41
3-year Sharpe Ratio	-0.46	0.74	1.21

Their total returns for the last ten years are First State 14.68%, Henderson 63.64% and United Global Healthcare fund 107.64%.

My opinion: Investors with a higher risk tolerance, a longer time frame, or are very bullish and optimistic on certain sectors, should go ahead and invest in sector UT. I would advise investors to also use the DCA method of investing for sector and thematic UTs to smooth out the volatility (*see* chapter 6.2).

From the chart below, we can see the volatility of sector UTs, especially First State Global Resources and United Global Healthcare fund. It is possible for sector UTs to deliver returns of 40% to 60% a year like United Global Healthcare in 2013–14 (in line with US equities strong recovery in 2013) and First State Global Resources in 2007–08 (where inflation was a very big concern). Exit strategies and the question of when to take profit is especially important for this category of UT. If not, it is also possible for the UTs to drop >10% in a month and slump further when the support level of individual shares in the UT holdings is broken (like First State Global Resources in second half of 2008 to the start of 2009).

9.9 Integration of different UT categories into one chart

I have taken one of the better funds from each of the subsections above (except for Thematic UT because there are just too many different themes in thematic UT category) and plotted them into a chart over the last three, five and ten years. It is clear that all the funds provided a positive return despite the two major challenges in the last decade the 2008 global financial crisis and the Eurozone debt crisis in 2010).

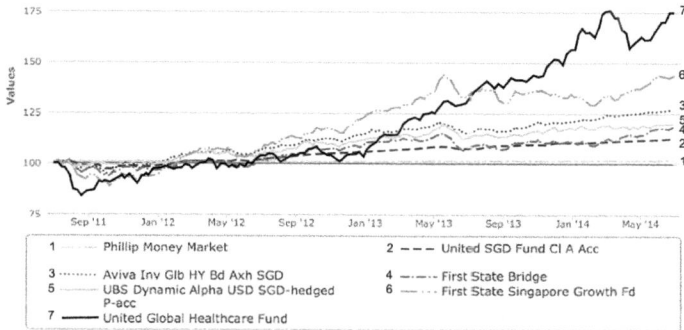

1 —— Phillip Money Market
2 – – – United SGD Fund Cl A Acc
3 ········ Aviva Inv Glb HY Bd Axh SGD
4 —·—·– First State Bridge
5 —— UBS Dynamic Alpha USD SGD-hedged P-acc
6 —— ··· First State Singapore Growth Fd
7 —— United Global Healthcare Fund

Fund Name	Annualised Returns	3 yr Annualised Volatility	Min NAV (SGD)	Max NAV (SGD)	Current NAV (SGD)
Phillip Money Market	0.5%	0.03	1.143	1.160	1.160 (07/07/2014)
United SGD Fund Cl A Acc	4.12%	2.08	1.459	1.698	1.698 (04/07/2014)
Aviva Inv Glb HY Bd Axh SGD	8.15%	6.7	9.738	11.468	11.269 (04/07/2014)
First State Bridge	5.79%	7.92	1.284	1.514	1.509 (04/07/2014)
UBS Dynamic Alpha USD SGD-hedged P-acc	6.23%	4.88	85.610	105.700	105.070 (04/07/2014)
First State Singapore Growth Fd	12.93%	12.31	2.046	3.392	3.392 (04/07/2014)
United Global Healthcare Fund	21.08%	13.32	1.477	3.174	3.174 (03/07/2014)

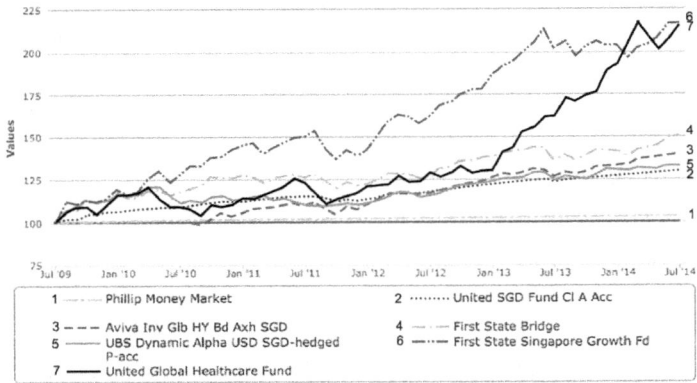

Fund Name	Annualised Returns	3 yr Annualised Volatility	Min NAV (SGD)	Max NAV (SGD)	Current NAV (SGD)
Phillip Money Market	0.61%	0.03	1.126	1.160	1.160 (07/07/2014)
United SGD Fund Cl A Acc	5.29%	2.08	1.313	1.698	1.698 (04/07/2014)
Aviva Inv Glb HY Bd Axh SGD	8.15%	6.7	9.738	11.468	11.269 (04/07/2014)
First State Bridge	8.54%	7.92	1.157	1.514	1.509 (04/07/2014)
UBS Dynamic Alpha USD SGD-hedged P-acc	5.99%	4.88	76.790	105.700	105.070 (04/07/2014)
First State Singapore Growth Fd	17.19%	12.31	1.513	3.392	3.392 (04/07/2014)
United Global Healthcare Fund	17.5%	13.32	1.422	3.174	3.174 (03/07/2014)

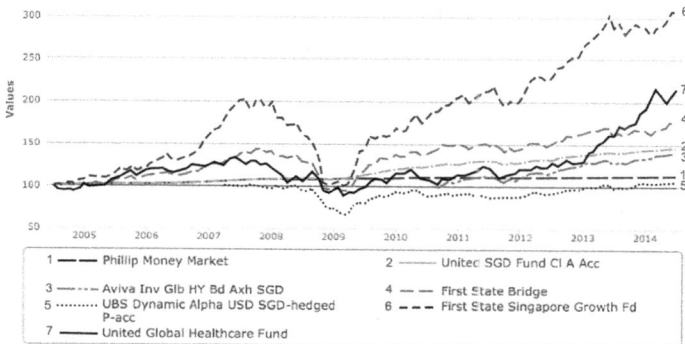

1 ——— Phillip Money Market	2 ——— Unitec SGD Fund Cl A Acc
3 ——··— Aviva Inv Glb HY Bd Axh SGD	4 —— First State Bridge
5 ·········· UBS Dynamic Alpha USD SGD-hedged P-acc	6 — — — First State Singapore Growth Fd
7 ——— United Global Healthcare Fund	

Fund Name	Annualised Returns	3 yr Annualised Volatility	Min NAV (SGD)	Max NAV (SGD)	Current NAV (SGD)
Phillip Money Market	1.15%	0.03	1.000	1.160	1.160 (07/07/2014)
United SGD Fund Cl A Acc	3.86%	2.08	1.171	1.698	1.698 (04/07/2014)
Aviva Inv Glb HY Bd Axh SGD	8.15%	6.7	9.738	11.468	11.269 (04/07/2014)
First State Bridge	8.54%	7.92	0.918	1.548	1.509 (04/07/2014)
UBS Dynamic Alpha USD SGD-hedged P-acc	5.99%	4.88	61.280	105.700	105.070 (04/07/2014)
First State Singapore Growth Fd	11.96%	12.31	1.041	3.392	3.392 (04/07/2014)
United Global Healthcare Fund	8.33%	13.32	1.198	3.174	3.174 (03/07/2014)

A couple of lessons we can draw from the charts above are:

1. Don't put all your eggs in one basket: diversify across different categories of UT is important as each category has different characteristics of performance at different periods of the economic cycle.
2. Time in the market vs timing the market: with a longer investment time horizon, an investor can ride through the roughest of waves.
3. Do not count your chickens before they hatch: Just like the earlier First State Global Resources fund, until the investor has confirmed the switch or sell trade, all profits are just paper gains.

Key learning points

• There are eight broad categories of UT, each with different investment objectives, holdings and performances.

- Investors must understand a couple of UTs from each category to build their dream portfolio and increase their chances to get consistent positive returns, especially if they are doing their own investment.

- Useful ratios to compare UT performance are AER, RRR and Sharpe Ratio on top of looking at the annualised returns and volatility. The min, max NAV in the period or since inception vs current NAV will give investors a good indication of whether current NAV is a bit high or low.

- For a thorough analysis, it is good to compare, in the same chart, the performance of shortlisted UTs of different fund houses and different categories of UTs for as long a period as there is sufficient data.

Endnotes

19. The STI took 48 months and 18 days to edge up from 1,588.36 (23 Sept 2003) to 3,875.77. I choose 23 Sept 2003 because its closing point was lower than 27 Feb 2009. Experienced investors remark that when markets move up, it is like taking a slow upward escalator but when markets plunge, it is akin to taking a free falling lift.
20. Housing Development Board, the Singapore government subsidized public housing scheme.

Factors that Affect Unit Trust Performance

After understanding the different categories of UT, we shall discuss the factors that impact on their performance. This will aid readers in understanding the reasons and external factors that will affect the performance and NAV of a UT.

10.1 Macroeconomic

Macroeconomic risks are broad factor risks that affect a large portion of the population in the economy. These factors include unemployment, economic output, inflation, savings, etc.

10.1.1 Global contagion risks

One of the biggest risks is global contagion risks, where financial problems in a country will spread rapidly to other countries like an epidemic (e.g., of the 1997 Asian financial crisis, 2008 global financial crisis and 2010 Eurozone debt crisis). This is particularly important as the financial systems of developed and developing economies are now more interdependent and interlinked than ever.

We can see how interlinked the global economy is from the Chinese government's lending to the US government for the purchase of their bonds and treasury bills in the last decade. In December 2000, China had held just $60.3 billion in US treasury and it swelled to $1.317 trillion in November 2013. That is an increase of 21.8 times in the last 13 years!

Another example is the Euro, introduced on 1 Jan 1999, gaining popularity in 1 Jan 2002. When more countries come together to use a common currency, their economies and financial markets will be more interlinked. (Stronger EU economies like Germany and France will feel more obliged to give financial aid to weaker economies like Greece and Portugal now that they use a common currency). Just like marrying into a big family, one's in-laws', parents' and siblings' health and financial matters also become a concern and everyone is expected to chip in to help when there is a crisis.

If there are increasing fears and pessimism in the global economy or one of the major international currencies faces a meltdown, the event will send shockwaves to financial systems worldwide and UT prices will not be spared. The popular saying "When USA sneezes, the world catches a cold" is very apt. If both the USA and China sneeze concurrently, investors worldwide will be gripped by fear!

10.1.2 Market Cycle Risks

This refers to the traditional phases of an economic or business cycle and different phases will affect prices of different categories of UTs. The four phases are "recovery", "expansion", "crisis", and "recession".

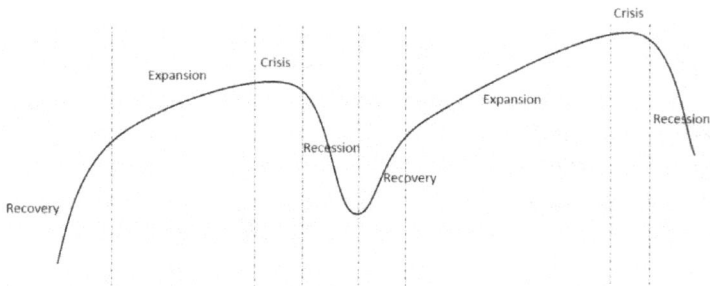

Recovery

Also known as the early cycle phase where government and central banks have very accommodat:ve fiscal (increasing government spending, lowering corporate and individual tax rates, etc.) and monetary policies (increasing money supply and lowering interest rates, etc.) to stimulate economic growth and activity (GDP, industrial production, employment and incomes increases). The early recovery phase is the best time to reallocate *more* investments from MM and short duration bonds UT to high yield UT, alternatives UT, equity UT and sector UT.

In the recovery phase, after the first hint of a turnaround of the economy, *financial* and *consumer discretionary* sectors will do exceptionally well because of low interest rates and an easing money supply environment. With the low interest rates, coupled with price discounts because of excess stockpile from the previous recession phase, many consumers may be tempted to spend again and increase their borrowings to purchase more luxury goods like cars, high-end residential units, higher priced consumer durables, etc. Financials may also see an improvement in their loans and businesses books.

Other sectors that will do well include *IT,* because of improving business optimism with higher anticipated consumer and corporate spending, demand for semiconductor chips and equipments used to produce other goods are likely to rise; as well as *industrials and materials,* because of the increase demand for packaging and transportat:on as trade rises. The sectors that will lag behind in the early phase tend to be defensive sectors like *telcos* and *utilities*; it is not that share prices of companies in this sector will drop but that their rates of increase will lag behind most sectors. The *energy* sector will lag too as inflation is not too big a concern at this point and energy prices tend to be lowered to spur economic production.

Expansion

Also known as the middle and longest of the four phases, there is still growth in the economy at this point, albeit at a slower pace. Company profits and economic growth seems to reach a peak. Monetary and fiscal policies are tighter now compared to the recovery phase as governments are becoming increasingly concerned with inflation. Increase in prices of most categories of UT can still be seen, although at a slower pace. In this phase investors will tend to make more money in riskier categories of UTs, but must be mindful of the rally ending soon and must plan to take profit from certain UTs and reallocate them to balanced and high-yield UTs.

In the expansion phase, the *IT* sector is likely to be one of the leading performers, as companies are more willing to spend on software, hardware and applications. The *industrials* sector will continue to fare well as businesses and economies are still expanding. Some major industrial giants and airlines will perform very well in periods of sustained economic growth. The *utilities* sector usually lags behind in the expansion phase as general demand for utilities is not dependent on the rate of growth of the economy. The *materials* sector will also lag because demand will be moderate and prices are not that high in this phase.

Crisis

This is the late phase of the market cycle. Prices tend to reach a peak and many exchanges report record high closing. Monetary and fiscal policies have become even more contractionary than the recovery phase due to fears of higher inflationary pressures. A handful of investors will still invest lump sum during this period as they see stocks and indexes setting record high; they rush to catch the last train, thinking there is still more profit to be made. Investors should shift their monies back to MM and short duration bonds UT to avoid getting badly hit when the markets take the inevitable nosedive.

In the crisis phase, inflationary pressures are being felt and the prices of raw goods will rise, hence *energy* and *materials* sectors will outperform others. Defensive sectors like *utilities, consumer staples* and *healthcare* also enjoy growth over other sectors because most investors will shift their monies to invest in less economically sensitive sectors that will still see demand regardless of the phases of the economic cycle.

The *consumer discretionary* sector will also lag because prices will be high now; it is increasingly more difficult to get credit approval and some consumers will postpone the consumption of luxury goods as interest rates and prices are high due to inflationary pressures. *IT* will also be an underperformer too as companies face increasing challenges to their corporate margins and slowing sales growth, as well as increased difficulty to obtain loans and credit facilities to expand their capital spending on technology.

Recession

This is the period of doom and gloom that most investors fear, save for a small group of investors will rejoice as they saw it coming. GDP drops, corporate profits decline, and credit and loans are hard to obtain. There is more fear of companies defaulting on their loans or becoming insolvent. Employees worry about retrenchment and keeping up with their obligations, and investors see a sea of red everyday when they log into the financial news or look at their portfolio. After several months of recession, it could be time for investors to think and gradually start to re-enter the market via regular monthly investing by selling off their MM and short duration bonds UT.

In this phase, almost all sectors of the economy will decline. *Consumer staples, utilities, telecoms* and *healthcare* are considered defensive sectors and less economically sensitive and might decline less. The demand for their goods and services tend to be more inelastic to prices. The sectors that are likely to lag more are the same as the crisis phase: the *consumer discretionary* and *IT* as well as *industrials* sector. This is because during the crisis phase the stockpiles add up as sales slows down. By the recession phase, the orders and business for industrials sector would be few and far between.

It is impossible to pinpoint exactly when markets reach the peak of the expansion cycle, or when markets absolutely bottom out in a recession. Hence a conscientious and savvy investor might ask the following questions. Given all the information on hand, which phase of the market cycle is the local and global economy in? Is the particular stock/UT or investment asset at this current price a 'fair value' compared to its historical price?

How much potential for upside[21] does the investment still have? What is the possible downside of price falling? What is my cut loss limit?[22]

10.1.3 Country risks

Investing in any country will carry some form of country-specific *social risks*. For example, the unrest in Bangkok from Nov 2013 to May 2014, which had their ruling party ousted from parliament, resulted in many months of lost productivity and reduced Thailand's GDP and its equity performance on their Stock Exchange of Thailand (SET).

Any UTs invested in single country Thailand or UTs with over 20% exposure to Thailand equities will be adversely affected because of the unrest.[23] Analysts also reported outflows of estimated US$3 billion from Thai stocks since late Nov 2013 to Feb 2014; some outflows were reinvested into other S.E.A stocks, the main beneficiary believed to be Indonesia shares with estimated US$192 million inflows traced from the sell-off in SET. Part of this could be attributed to UT fund managers managing Asia Pacific equities rebalancing their portfolio and geographical allocation to underweight Thai equities during this period and overweight other regional equities in Indonesia, Malaysia and Vietnam etc.

Political risks

Political changes in the government's and/or ruling party's policies may cause economic uncertainty and, depending on the policies passed, may be a good or bad thing for UTs investing in that country.

In the 2014 India Elections, the BJP (Bharatiya Janata Party) won a landslide victory.[24] Their political agenda was seen as more pro-business and driven towards development. Their policies included extensive privatisation of infrastructure and services and increased cutback on labour and environmental regulations, resulting in India's stock market rallying for a couple of weeks especially in their property sector. UTs that were invested in India equities performed likewise (*see* chart below especially the leap in May 2014 vs the STI). This chart also shows that news can move prices of companies rapidly and if investors are slow to take action, they will miss the opportunity. The NAV of Amundi India Infrastructure and HSBC Indian Equity both appreciated by more than 25% from May 8th to May 23rd in just 15 days or 10 trading days! This chart again shows that UTs managed by different fund house can have vastly different magnitude of returns although they share similar investment objectives and invest in the same country.

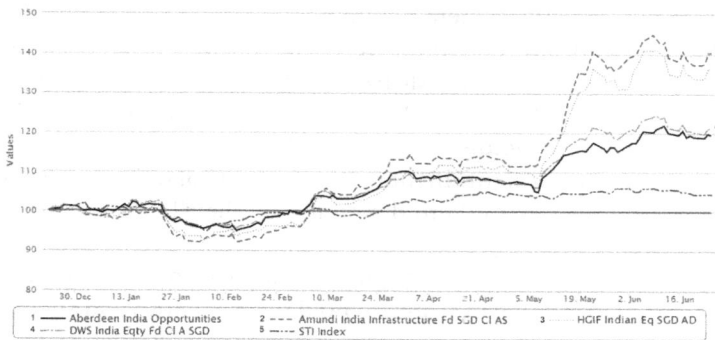

10.2 Other economic risks

I will present economic risks in these two types: non-human causes (forces of nature/Acts of God) and man-made causes (Central Bank passing Monetary policies).

An example of non-human cause of economic risks is the March 2011 Japan earthquake and resulting tsunami on the east coast Tohoku region, which damaged the Fukushima nuclear power plant reactors and released radioactive substances in the environment over a 20km radius.[25] The disaster also caused Japan's stock Index Nikkei 225 to drop over 10% in the second day of the disaster and the index to close -17% for the entire 2011 after investigations unfolded the full extent of damages and the impact of the earthquake on Japan's economy. Aberdeen Japan equity UT dropped about 10% in the month from Feb 2011 to Mar 2011 and ended the year 2011 at -6.97%.

Man-made causes of economic risks include central banks' intervention and control of interest rates. The levels of interest rates in any economy have a direct impact on almost all investment in the economy. When central banks want to stifle growth and economic activity, they can raise interest rates, and increase borrowing and financing costs for companies and individuals. As interest rates go up, yields on bonds need to rise to make it attractive for investors to buy the bonds; with higher bonds yields, bond prices will have to fall as they are inversely proportionate, and the longer the bond duration (longer than three years), the more sensitive it is to interest rate movements. This will affect mostly Bond UTs, especially those with longer average maturity in their holdings. UT Investors can find the average maturity in the factsheet or prospectus, if not they can ask their distributor or FAR for more information. High yield bond UTs will drop in NAV because, remember, most of the companies in its holdings are rated BBB and below, and higher interest rates will signal higher financial costs of doing business, increasing the risk of them defaulting on their loans and going bankrupt.

Balanced UT categories might have a lesser direct impact as UT fund managers can switch to hold more equities and shorter duration bonds in view of rising interest rates. Persistent high interest rates will make it more expensive for consumers to buy large ticket items like property and cars, and for businesses to obtain loans to buy machinery and other capital expansion; these parties may just decide not to spend which is bad for businesses and equity UTs in the long run. Higher interest rates can also incentivize a portion of the population to want to save more money and delay spending on big ticket items, which is bad for equities UT.

Central Banks can *regulate the bank's reserve ratio requirements*, to either hasten or slow the rate of growth in the economy. We all know the multiplier and spill-on effect of increased money supply in the economy causing more transactions. To adopt an expansionary or loose monetary policy, central banks can reduce the deposit requirements that banks need to keep liquid for every dollar of deposit they accept, resulting in the banks having more money to loan out and supply to the markets and make it easier and cheaper for businesses to obtain credit and financing. This is good for equities and NAV of equities UT might rise.

Central banks can also intervene in the economy by tweaking the foreign exchange rate.[26] Sharp currency movements will affect the overall performance and NAV of the UTs. If an investor had invested in a non SGD-hedged Thailand equity UT just before their social unrest in late 2013, the resulting slump in their Thai Baht and Thai equities would have caused the investor's capital to suffer a double whammy from both the equities drop as well as the depreciation of THB against the SGD in the period. In recent years, some UTs launched a separate share class for investors who like the investment objectives, holdings and geographical areas of the UT but not the currency outlook of the country hence they can opt for the SGD-Hedged share class (*see* section 2.5.7). With the hedged class, investor's fears of currency fluctuations affecting the UT's NAV will be minimised.

10.3 Sector Specific Risks

Every sector in the economy has its unique challenges and risks to manage, and there are risks that may affect a specific sector of the economy more than other sectors. For example, if Singapore's Ministry of Manpower passes a labour law restricting the number of foreign workers to local workers that companies can hire, sectors like the infrastructure, industrials and property will be more directly hit as they are traditionally more reliant on manpower. This may also lead to a firm's increased production costs and reduced competitiveness as they may need to hire more locals or have to outsource certain parts of the production overseas. Investors of UTs that are concentrated in these sectors may see the NAV fall because the prices of individual companies within the UT have dropped.

10.4 Non-economic factors

In my opinion, the *fund manager and team of analysts* is certainly the most important factor that affects a UT's performance. Working within the fund's investment objectives, they decide which companies to buy, when to buy, how long to hold, how much and when to sell. They are also responsible for executing derivatives and hedging strategies if the specific UT uses these tools.

The team has to be extremely competent and up-to-date on news and developments. They have to be specialists in their area of expertise: equities or bonds, geographical region, sector of the economy and investment theme for thematic UTs. They also need to be all-rounded in the other areas of politics, economics, world news, technology trends, etc.

I have heard of some UT management teams performing regular risk analytics and simulation scenarios to stress test their UT portfolio if certain events take place so they can constantly review their holdings and make better future investments. Their ultimate aim is to grow their fund size and attract more investment inflows as they are paid an annual management fee of 0.5% to 2% of the fund size. This is a small fee for investors to pay considering the team's expertise, commitment and value add they can give investors.

10.4.1 The expenses of the UT

It is natural that all investors do not like to pay fees when they invest as it reduces net returns. Unless the investor has better expertise than the fund management team and able to monitor the investments plus able to enjoy lower transaction costs due to economies of scale that a UT has by pooling resources of individual investors together, otherwise the individual investor may be better to pay fees and expenses to the professionals.

10.4.2 Financial derivatives

Some UTs use financial derivatives[27] to enhance returns to the investors or to limit the risk or reduce the volatility. Even if the UT managers do not use derivatives, it is common for some companies within the UT's holdings to use them to hedge against currency or commodity volatile prices. This is especially true for large MNCs or companies in the airlines and logistics industry with operations that rely on a single commodity like crude oil.

As Warren Buffett said, 'Derivatives are financial weapons of mass destruction and ticking time bombs especially derivatives combined with considerable leverage'. Investors should read the product highlight sheet and refer to the prospectus or ask their representative to find out more details about the derivatives of the UT, if any used by the UT managers before they invest.

10.4.3 Credit and default risks of companies

This applies to individual companies within the UT. If the company's credit rating is downgraded by ratings agency such as Moody's and S&P, the company's cost of borrowing will go up, leading to a drop in the company's share price as increased borrowing costs will push up expenses and see net profits drop.

If a company goes into default and cannot pay their loan interest and other borrowing costs, their credit rating and price will drop further. Any UT that has securities of this company will experience a drop in NAV. This also applies to UTs, especially in the high-yield category, if the UT is unable to pay out the monthly distributions to the unit holders for a prolonged period, many investors will lose faith and switch out or sell.

10.4.4 Non-compliance risks

These refer to risk of fund managers deviating away from the original investment objectives and other set out rules. Examples of these breaches include investing outside the geographical boundaries set out in the mandate, dabbling in derivatives not made known to the Trustee or not getting approval by the UT unit holders beforehand. It can even include fraudulent or dishonest acts by the UT Management team in an attempt to cover up and fail to report abnormalities to the Trustee.

Other kinds of breach associated with thematic UTs could be the UT manager investing in companies with business operations widely thought to be Shariah compliant for many years, only to know from recent investigations into the company's operations by the authorities proved otherwise. This will result in the price of the company dropping and thus the NAV of the UT will dip too. The UT manager will be forced to sell that company from their holdings at likely a much lower price than before as it is not Shariah compliant anymore.

Key learning points

- Macroeconomic factors that affect the performance of the UT include global contagion risks, market cycle risks, country risks, political risks, economic risks (natural causes and man make causes) and specific sector risks.

- Non-economic factors that affect the performance of the UT include the abilities of the fund manager and analyst team, expenses of the UT, financial derivatives used by the UT, credit and default risks of companies in the UT holdings and non-compliance risks.

- These common factors that will affect performance of UTs are not exhaustive, investors need to constantly monitor news for natural disasters or political unrest, etc., and central bank passing policies to see if they are heating up or cooling down the economy for geographical areas the investor is invested into. Also every time the UT fund managers do up a new monthly factsheet or when they make new announcements, investors should read and clarify if there is a doubt. By having these good habits, investors can react faster and either sell, switch or buy more UTs.

Endnotes

21. I.e., the likelihood of further increase in its price.
22. I.e., the maximum loss in percentage or amount that the investor is willing to lose.
23. Aberdeen Thailand UT declined 8.43% in the last quarter of 2013. The unrest created the most havoc for tourism, hospitality, local businesses and MNCs delayed their expansion plans or chose to invest their capital elsewhere. Reports also showed the Thai Baht weakened 4.6% in the first two months of unrest, the SET declined 9.1% over the same period and Thailand's 2014 GDP growth projection was cut from 4% to 3% too.
24. This was the first time in close to 30 years a single party achieved an outright majority of the seats in the lower house of the parliament of India. The previous time the party was in power (1999 to 2004), the country was more liberal and pro globalization; their leadership brought significant GDP growth to India's economy.
25. It was estimated the earthquake cost the Japanese economy an estimated US$212 billion as the Tohoku region was responsible for producing approx 10% of Japan's total machinery and electrical production and these are used

for Japan's exports to Indonesia, Malaysia, Thailand ard Philippines which had their supply chain disrupted. Toyota was the world's biggest automobile maker for years before the incident, and it slipped to third place behind GM and Volkswagen in the first half of 2011 as it had to shut 12 of its factories in Japan because of the Earthquake.

26. These directly impact the economy's currency to make it stronger or weaker, depending on whether the state wants to adopt an expansionary or contractionary monetary policy. Forex rates will affect the country's trading books, MNCs doing business in the country and even tourist arrivals, etc.

27. A derivative is an instrument that derives its performance from an underlying. In financial derivatives, the underlying could be a bond, an index, a company, a commodity or currencies and many other examples, as long as the underlying has a price and can be structured.

PART 3

Appendix

11

Appendix 1: Good Questions to Ask Your FAR

If you decide to buy UT via a representative, here is a list of questions that you can ask him or her. On top of helping you understand more about the UTs, some of the questions will help protect your interests and allow you to gauge the FAR's level of competence and experience.

Question #1: Is the recommended UT authorised/approved for sale in Singapore by a relevant body? Is it a legitimate UT?

UTs to be marketed and distributed in Singapore need to be registered with MAS to obtain approval. MAS have rules and regulations in place; for example, requiring the fund manager's investments to be liquid and diversified. MAS also checks whether the disclosures in the fund's prospectus, product highlight sheets and factsheets are true and accurate to enable interested investors to make an informed decision before purchasing.

The MAS approval for sale of the UT or any investments does not guarantee their performance or profitability. Investors must consider and weigh the pros and cons and risks of the investments themselves. I will warn investors to stay away from companies placed on the MAS investor alert list[28] and also any companies or individuals conducting unregulated investment schemes[29] that other victims fell prey for. Before they part away with their hard earned money, they can google for MAS investor alert list and MAS unregulated schemes and read through the contents thoroughly.

Question #2: Is the FAR representing a regulated financial institution?

When investors buy from a MAS-regulated financial institution, they have the assurance that MAS can investigate if there are any wrongdoings and take regulatory actions against the institutions that have breached MAS rules and regulations versus an unregulated institution or company. Investors can do a quick internet search for MAS-regulated financial institution to find the company names of registered and relevant organisations,[30] it even has money changers, remittance, finance Companies, etc. It is highly advisable to check this list first before doing money and finance related business with any Singapore company.

Most regulated Financial Institutions also belong to associations like the Association of Banks in Singapore (ABS), Life Insurance of Singapore (LIA), etc and they normally will adhere to a service standard of getting back to the customer within a maximum period of usually two to three weeks.

At the time of writing, over 380 regulated financial institutions in Singapore have subscribed to Financial Industry Disputes Resolution Centre Ltd (FIDReC and agreed to submit to FIDReC's jurisdiction in adjudicating complaints brought against them by consumers. FIDReC was launched in May 2005 to provide an affordable alternative dispute resolution scheme that is independent and impartial so as to encourage and assist in resolution of disputes between consumers and financial institutions in an amicable and fair manner.

Question #3: How long has the FAR been in this industry and how he/she can help me?

Potential investors can ask their representative how long they have been in the business, why they decided to join this industry and what are their career future goals. It is important to find out about the representative's current experience in managing UTs and how they intend to achieve the investor's goals from the UTs. Through the conversation, or after multiple meetings with this particular representative, potential investors can get a feel of whether there is a correct 'fit' between the FAR and investor, and like all good relationships, time will tell if it works.

When investors purchase UTs through a licensed FAR, they can be assured that he or she has attained the minimum entry requirements and passed relevant examinations. Representatives are also required to clock at least 33 hours (current standards) of annual training to keep their knowledge and skills up-to-date, and pass competency examinations to adhere to business conduct rules and standards.

Question #4: How is the recommended UT able to meet my objectives?

The FAR must be able to demonstrate how the recommended UT will confer benefits within an acceptable range of risk that the investor can tolerate to meet the investor's objectives. If the FAR is unclear on the explanation or the recommended UT does not seem to be in line with the objectives of the investor, always revisit the fact find stage, which is the goal setting process where the FAR asks the investor questions like his/her goals and time horizon, current assets and liabilities, risk profile, past investment experience, current investments still on hand, etc.

Question #5: What is the commitment amount and time for this UT?

The investor should also ask the representative the amount that he/she needs to commit as well as the frequency, whether it is a one-off lump sum, monthly investments or a combination of both, and for how long is the recommended time horizon for the investments.

Question #6: What are the various fees and charges for this investment?

This is an important question so the investor will not be in for a rude shock when he/she receives the statements. The types of fees that are commonly charged for Singapore UTs have been discussed in Section 2.7. Do ask whether there are costs and fees over and above the fees that are not included in Section 2.7.

Question #7: What are other alternatives if I do not purchase this UT?

Potential investors can ask their FAR if there are other UTs or other alternative wealth instruments that will also be able to address their objectives within their risk tolerance and time horizon. This is important to reduce post investment regret especially when markets are volatile, the investor can stay the course and be less emotional remembering at the point of investing, other UTs and alternative wealth instruments was researched and shared by the FAR.

Question #8: If I do purchase the UT, how do I receive updates on its performance? Where can I find them?

At the point where the UT is proposed, the investor must be given a copy of the UT's specific fund factsheet, product highlight sheet and prospectus (*see* chapter 8). The documents will help them make a more informed decision before they decide to invest.

If the investor goes ahead, he or she needs to ask the representative how and where to get the updates on the fund performance to know if his/her goals are still on track. There are two kinds of updates online or print. Clients can log into their individual account online to view their portfolio performance, or obtain the latest prices of the UTs from the website of the distributor they purchased the UT from. They are also likely to receive hardcopy statements mailed to them either quarterly or monthly if they perform monthly RSP or reinvest their monthly dividends. Another source of print would be the financial section in mainstream local newspapers.

Keep up to date and read quarterly articles on the performance, fund inflow reports, risk reporting reports of UTs especially those included under the CPFIS.[31] The reports are jointly produced by Lipper, a global leader in supplying mutual fund information and fund ratings.

Question #9: How liquid is the UT redemption? How long do I have to wait to get my money back?

This is an important question for investors to ask when they want to sell or switch their UTs, in other words, what is the cut-off time if they want to secure the same day closing price as well as the steps to make the sell transactions. For most UT distributors, if the investor can approve the sales transaction online or they make a trip to the UT distributor's office before 1pm, they will likely be able to sell on that same day with prices known one business day later since UTs NAV are forward pricing.

For investors doing a sell transaction via hardcopy forms submitted through their representatives, it may take between two to three working days before the sales transaction is put through. The delay of a few days can be very significant, especially in a market recessionary phase when fear overtakes logic and reasoning and is possible for UTs to drop between 1–3% per day when the broad index falls by 3–4%.

Investors should also ask their representatives about the waiting time between selling the investments to getting the proceeds in a cheque or direct credit into their bank accounts. The standard turnaround time is between 10 to 12 working days for most UT distributors.

Question #10: If I change my mind about the investment, is there a cancellation period? Will there be any charges?

Most UT distributors will allow for a cancellation period (known as "free-look") of seven working days from the date of purchase if it is a UT that the investor has never bought with the particular distributor before.

For cancellation requests, the sales charge/upfront fee will be refunded back to the investor. However any losses due to a drop in NAV of the funds from the purchase date to the date the distributor receives the cancellation request will be borne by the investor. Conversely, the investor will not be able to earn from the gains should there be an increase in the NAV of the UT between the purchase date to the cancellation date, the distributor retains the profit.

Endnotes

28 http://www.mas.gov.sg/MoneySENSE/Understanding-Financial-Products/
Investments/Investor-Alert-List/IAL-Listing.aspx?sc_p=all
29 http://www.mas.gov.sg/MoneySENSE/Understanding-Financial-Products/
Investments/Consumer-Alerts.aspx#cus
30 https://masnetsvc.mas.gov.sg/FID.html
31 A good and free online platform is www.fundsingapore.com, a joint
collaboration between Investment Management Association of Singapore
(IMAS) and Life Insurance Association of Singapore (LIA). Fundsingapore.com
is not a UT distributor, thus resources and articles on the website are often
seen as pretty objective and unbiased.

12

Appendix 2: Interview with Wong Sui Jau

Retirement Ambassador, iFAST Finarcial Ltd

Mr Wong Sui Jau was born in 1974. He graduated in 1998 with a Bachelors of Accountancy from Nanyang Technological University. He then joined Pricewaterhouse Coopers in 1998 and worked as a tax consultant for more than two years. In 2000, he joined iFAST Financial as Senior Analyst and was appointed Research Manager in April 2003. Subsequently, he was appointed General Manager of Fundsupermart in August 2005 to Dec 2014. His current appointment is Retirement Ambassador at iFAST Financial Ltd. Sui Jau's investment views have been featured on various local and international media, including Bloomberg, Channel NewsAsia, CNBC, Lianhe Zaobao, Radio FM 93.8, *etc.*

What are some challenges running a UT platform?

Firstly, the downward pressure of prices. Due to competition, sales charges have been consistently lowered time and again over the years despite increased services and product offerings. Secondly, there is increased regulation today. The global financial crisis resulted in many new regulations being passed to protect investors, as well as tightened money laundering and technical risk requirements. Systems and procedures all need to be changed for all these requirements to be adhered to; while they may sometimes result in some inconvenience to investors, they are necessary. All these compliance measures and tighter regulations increase our operating costs and pose challenges to our profit margins further. Lastly, we have had to adapt to new mediums. Social media has taken off in a big way, as have apps from smart phones. When the internet become popular in the '90s, Fundsupermart was at the forefront of that change. We have to ensure we embrace the new mediums now as well.

What is your personal take on investing in unit trusts, any tips for investors to select the right ones to make money consistently ? What is your investment portfolio like?

My personal take is that the unit trust is a great way to learn about investing, and it can be used as one of the primary instruments for investing throughout one's life. I have made over $200,000 in more than 18 years through several market cycles, ups and downs, so I can attest that with patience, unit trusts can certainly serve as a good investment tool. I believe in regular investing and saving a portion of my pay cheque incrementally when I get bonuses and pay increments. Hence over the course of my working life, I have squirrelled away and invested slightly over $500,000 in capital.

It is important to start investing young and learn from your mistakes. Investing is like a journey, so it is more important to learn as much as you can from your experiences rather than focus on any one single investment decision at a single point in time.

My unit trust portfolio can be found on my investment blog on Fundsupermart: https://secure.fundsupermart.com/main/ community/Portfolio_View.svdo?pid=P11762

What do you think of Singapore's future UT landscape, the next 10–20 years for the parties involved particularly investors, platform providers and distributors?

There will be many more investment options available to investors in the next 10 to 20 years. Platforms providers like Fundsupermart will become more important because investors want a neutral place for objective and consolidated information.

Upfront costs will continue to come down, and will reach zero at some point.

You make a lot of media appearances every year. How did you become the respected 'go to' guy for advice on investing in unit trusts and financial markets? Any tips?

I started in this industry in iFAST's research team as a senior research analyst. From the very start, due to the nature of unit trusts, which are usually invested for time periods of up to three years or longer, we agreed that we would take a longer term view towards markets. Hence, we filtered out a lot of the short-term noise. During large sell downs or market crisis, we are often the voice of calm asking investors not to panic. We have also tended to be earlier in calling a market cheap once it has sold off to a certain level. I believe investors and the media remember that after the crisis is over. Similarly, we don't always like the hot sectors. There was times when a particular investment was really popular (like gold a few years back), but we are not afraid to come out and say we don't like this or that.

Who are your favourite investors of all time, especially those whose knowledge and teachings have an influence on your work and why so? Any favourite investment quotes?

Warren Buffet, a value driven investor, and the most successful investor in the world. Peter Lynch is a well-known ex fund manager who wrote a book called *One Up on Wall Street*. He talks about noticing things in daily life and transforming these insights into investment ideas. My favourite quote is from Baron Rothschild, an eighteenth-century British nobleman and member of the Rothschild banking family, credited with saying that "The time to buy is when there's blood in the streets."

Lastly, what are some of your favourite books or online journals you recommend investors read?

One Up on Wall Street by Peter Lynch. This was one of the first investment books I read, and it was also one of the books that inspired me to learn about investing (by myself) and to make a career change and join iFAST. Although the focus is on stocks, the book was also inspirational in the sense that it addresses spotting investment trends in everyday life, how stock markets work, and keeping an open mind on new ideas. Since a large part of my investment knowledge was initially self-taught, this book was also great because it was simple to read and was not filled with technical jargon.

Another book I'd recommend is *The Millionaire Next Door: Surprising Secrets of American's Wealthy* by Thomas J. Stanley and William D. Danko. This is also another inspirational book. It shows that even that humble couple next door, who might not be earning that much, can still be millionaires due to their humble lifestyle and savvy investing and spending habits.

From left to right: Wee Kiong, Sui Jau, and Derek

13

Appendix 3: Interview w th Apelles Poh

Financial Advisory Branch Director

Mr Apelles Poh is the author of the national bestseller Live Well, Love Much, Laugh Often, *an inspirational book titled and is one of the most respected Financial Adviser Representatives (FAR) in the financial services industry. He is also the principal trainer at Eagle's Wings Training & Consultancy, a training company that he set up to impact lives through the spoken word. He has a sizable AUA (Assets under Advice) from his 23 years of working in this industry. He has also qualified for MDRT for 11 consecutive years with another four years of COT and five years of TOT, representing the top 1% of financial planners in the world. To learn more about Apelles and his passion and work, you can visit his website at http://www.apellespoh.com/.*

You are very successful in your profession, how do you keep this passion going?

I feel blest to be in this industy as I am a people-person by nature. After a while, clients became friends and I get involved with their lives, like attending weddings and baby showers and even spending time with them when they are hospitalised. I am also a qualified counsellor so besides financial planning advice, sometimes I also coach and counsel my clients on family and work issues. On the aspect of financial planning, I always believe in educating the client in doing holistic planning and recommending suitable products to address their concerns—very much like a doctor who needs to do a diagnosis before giving the prescription. I enjoy what I do and I know what I do can make a difference and that's why I am so passionate in my calling.

Can you share the most remarkable investment returns that you have helped a single client achieve?

Instead of a single client, I like to share that a number of my clients who have been with me for more than ten years have about doubled their investments and achieved a good return on their UTs. The joy I get is the confidence they placed in me in keeping their investments through bad times like the global financial crisis and even topping up when the markets are down. I do not advocate a trading strategy but rather an accumulation strategy for my clients in say, planning for their retirement. I mean, we don't want to 'trade' away our retirement pot on a wrong bet on the markets, right?

Have you noticed any changes in the Singapore unit trusts landscape over the last 20 years?

I have seen the introduction of UT platforms that came up in the last 15 years. This has helped me to monitor my client's portfolio more effectively and to do switches online and on time with excellent IT support, like what iFAST Financial (the platform) is providing. Clients can also approve their trades online when they are overseas with the UT platforms. In the late nineties when I started with investment-linked products, there was no such technology available. Every trade was done using pen and paper. Can you imagine the time lapse when you have to rebalance or switch funds for many clients at one go?

What is your personal take on Unit Trusts?

I believe in UTs and I think is a good instrument for people to save towards retirement. There is diversification and active management, and one can invest with as little as $1,000, even in stocks or bonds in China, Europe or the United States. However,

UTs are long-term investment instruments (longer than five years) and the charges are generally higher than ETFs and direct shares investment. However, UTs are just one asset class that I have. Others include properties, insurance policies and shares.

Can you share more on your personal investment portfolio and your investment strategy for unit trusts?

A dentist should have good teeth in order to give credible advice. Therefore I have been investing in UTs for about 15 years and I usually hold them unless there are fundamental changes in the funds. I also believe in dollar cost averaging as it is hard to time the markets correctly all the time. Having time in the markets works wonderfully when you can regularly buy into it (even when it is down).

What is one common mistake you have observed investors making?

One common mistake is that investors tend to panic and overreact whenever there is bad news. Bad news create fear and this is amplified and magnified especially when it is constantly on the headlines of newspapers. I would urge investors to think calmly and rationally and not to be swayed only by emotions. If not, one will tend to buy high (good news) and sell low (bad news). Learn from the legendary billionaire investor Warren Buffet, "Be greedy when others are fearful, and be fearful when others are greedy".

You are managing your clients' monies, how do you keep up with daily financial news and choose good UTs?

I spend about 30 minutes to an hour daily reading news and looking at financial websites just to keep updated with what is going on in the world. Occasionally I will attend fund managers' briefings to sieve out funds that are worth investing in. We have to keep updated or we will become outdated. However, we must remember that investing in UTs is long term in nature, and it is unwise to have a knee-jerk reaction to everything that is happening in the news and markets.

How do you ride through the storm with your clients, especially in volatile and turbulent phases in the markets?

I educate clients on the Three Pots of Money Concept : Pot A is their emergency and short-term cash pot, Pot B is their medium to long-term pot (which I will help them manage and invest into UTs and other financial instruments) and Pot C is the speculative pot (these are instruments used for trading and I tell clients not to dabble into it unless they know what they are getting into.) During the crisis, I reminded clients that their monies in UTs are for the medium to long-term (ten years or longer), for example, planning for their retirement. Sentiments should improve after each crisis as we saw the markets rebounded after the Asian financial crisis in 1997 and the global financial crisis in 2008. The most important thing during a crisis is that you must stay in touch with your clients, meet up with them, and update them on the situation. It is sad that there were some planners I know who dropped out during the 2008 global financial crisis.

Any practical examples of helping clients, maybe during the 2000 dot.com bubble burst or the 2008 global financial frisis?

I believe a good financial planner will need three types of skills in managing a client's portfolio: Funds management skills, relationship management skills and crisis management skills. The first is the ability to analyse and recommend suitable funds and create a portfolio based on the risk profile, time horizon and financial situation of the clients. Second is the ability to relate to our clients, that is, to manage the non-business part of the business. Third is the need to be there in touch with our clients during a financial crisis. In 2008, in the midst of the Lehman and global financial crisis, we organised a number of seminars for our clients and even engaged a psychologist to give talks to encourage our clients as some of them had lost their jobs. We need to understand their stress and empathize with them. I remembered almost every weekend for six months, I spent time with my clients over lunch or dinner and provided them with advice and support. Our team also sent out a lot of updates, emails and SMSes proactively to our clients. It is like the captain of a plane giving you updates and assurance when the plane is going through a turbulence. This will be most helpful to calm the jittery nerves of our clients.

In your opinion, how much UTs advice is an art form and how much is science?

I think it is 50% art and 50% science. It is an art because as a financial planner, we need good communication and connecting skills (e.g. the ability to tell stories to make complex concepts simple to understand). We also need to build and nurture our relationship with our clients over time. I think this is the emotional quotient or EQ part of our advice.

The 50% science is the technical knowledge of how markets and funds behave and how to put together a portfolio of funds for the client. I think this is the intelligence quotient or IQ part of our advice.

Do you think there is a difference between having an investor select the UTs independently and getting a FAR to do it?

If investors have the know-how and the discipline and can keep in check their emotions when investing, then they can and should invest on their own. However, having a FAR has its advantages. Beside creating a suitable portfolio, a good FAR can also provide holistic planning advice like insurance planning, will writing, lasting power of attorney etc. More importantly, the FAR can be the steadying hand to the rudder of the ship when there is a financial storm. Together with their clients, they can go through the bumps in the storm and reach their clients' objective. Often without a FAR, investors may be tempted to sell down their funds in the thick and thin of a financial crisis.

Do you have any tips or words of advice for the readers to build a portfolio of unit trusts for their objectives?

Instead of tips of which funds are good, let me give a broader picture on the 7-steps of financial planning which I also covered in my second book *Facts Tell, Stories Sell*:

Step 1 – Maintain a Budget

There should be positive cash-flows – income minus expenses

and debt-repayment – on a regular basis. This excess cash flow can be saved or invested for the future. This simple step is perhaps the most fundamental and the most challenging to many.

The obsession with some people for materials things, for the latest gadgets, toys and accessories can detrail even the best laid financial plan. Excessive present consumption can ruin our future aspirations. Such behaviours stem from one's personal belief system and values in life and about life. Our thinking produces our feelings, and our feelings produce our doings, that is, our actions. And our belief system and values come from the people we meet, the books we read, the media we visit and the past experiences we keep.

Be aware and be careful to adopt and adapt to values that will help you rather than hinder you in life. Strike a balance between current consumption and delayed gratification. Look around you – successful people in any field of endeavors have mastered this most crucial factor to their success, that is, the power of delayed gratification. If you want to retire young and retire rich, then this should of utmost importance in your agenda. Learn to live below your means; and not beyond or at your means. A dollar saved and invested is a dollar multiplied.

Step 2 – Keep an Emergency Fund

There should be at least three to six months of income in a liquid bank account for emergency purposes. The self-employed and retirees should have more than 6 months of emergency cash.

Step 3 – Save for Short-term Needs

Anything that we may need in the short term of between one to three years should not be invested into risky instruments but should be put into a savings / fixed deposits/ money markets. Some people would also set aside a portion of money here to be used as an Opportunity Fund, in case there are good investment opportunities that may arise in the short term.

Step 4 – Risk Management

Once you have taken care of the first three steps, you need to manage the risks that can threaten you and your family's life, lifestyle and future. Areas to look out for are death, total permanent disability and critical illness coverage including mortgage protection, hospitalization reimbursement (Shield plans), disability income and long-term care (Eldershield), personal accident, travel, and home content insurances. If you are running a business, then certain more specialized planning like keyman, partnership insurance and business disruption insurance may be needed.

Surely, insurance is a need, not a want or a luxury. Sometimes, when I hear people say they can't afford insurance, I tell them that they can't afford *not* to have insurance. It is unfair and unwise to risk our loved ones' future because we have neglected this important area of planning. The Chinese have this saying "Bu pa yi wan, zhi pa wan yi", which translates to "You should be prepared, just in case". This is certainly true.

Step 5 – Investment Planning

This is where you put your hard-earned money to work harder for you. Investment is a necessity because of the problem of inflation. Saving money in the bank is not investing because it would likely be eaten up by inflation in the long run. Normally I use some of the pointers below as a form of education for clients:

- Diversification – Don't put all your eggs in one basket. Studies have shown that asset allocation is a major contribution of returns in a portfolio.

- Time / Patience – Time, and not timing, is the key. It is very difficult to time the market correctly all the time. Most investments need a longer time of more than five years to see the fruits.

- Risk / Reward – The higher the risk, the greater the potential reward. Not taking risks (for example, bank deposit) is itself a very great risk, that is, the risk of inflation eroding the value of our money.

- Dollar Cost Averaging – Invest regularly. This will be to our advantage even if markets go down ,and it will.

- Prudence – Invest only after you have set aside money for your emergency funds and short term needs (one to three years).

- Expectation – Markets may be volatile and may drop say, 30% percent or more due to a crisis, for example, 9/11, SARS. You must not panic because history shows us that they will recover. In fact, in a diversified portfolio, a good time to buy is after a crisis.

Step 6 – Education and Retirement Planning

These are more specific needs that we can use – shares, unit-trusts, ETFs, endowment policies –to fund and plan. For a child's tertiary education planning, the use of endowment plans (though generally endowment plans have lower returns vis-à-vis investment in the long term) with an Enhanced Payor Benefit would be ideal. This will ensure that there is money for the child's education even if the payor or the parent is "not around" or is unable to fund the premiums due to a critical illness.

Factors to consider in retirement planning include the monthly income desired at retirement, the number of years to retirement, the number of years in retirement, the investment rate of return, the inflation rate, the risk profile and the amount –lump-sums and regular – that have been set aside for retirement planning. When you retire, it is not how much you have earned that matters. What matters is how much you have saved and invested.

Another good question to ponder is "What are you doing during your two-thirds of working adult life, for your one-third of non-working adult life?" With reducing mortality, the danger is that we can last longer than our money. A recent *Straits Times* article said that Singaporeans are the fourth longest living people in the world. The average Singaporean man lives up to eighty years of age, while the average Singaporean woman lives up to eighty-five years of age. Just imagine, you could be living for thirty years on no-pay leave. Time and tide wait for no man. You know you are getting old when your bones can tell the weather. You know you are really getting old when your teeth are sleeping separately from you. Therefore, make sure your golden years are golden, not grey. Start planning now. The silver tsunami is coming but it is also a golden opportunity for financial planners to swing into action.

Step 7 – Tax, Estate and Legacy Planning

Singapore has a relatively easy-to-understand personal tax system. There are a few ways whereby an individual can reduce the tax burden. These include making contributions to the Supplementary Retirement Scheme, increasing the CPF contribution by a self-employed, using cash to top up CPF Special/ Retirement account and via donations to Institutions of public character. (Visit the CPF website for details.)

For estate planning, you should make sure that your estate, what you leave behind after your passing, goes to the right party in the shortest possible time, with the least possible loss. It is good news that death taxes are abolished in Singapore.

Basic provisions include writing a will, doing the necessary nominations, titling your property and assets correctly, getting enough coverage so the estate would not be subjected to losses and creditors. For the wealthier, trusts may be created so that the wishes of the deceased can be maintained for the longer term. Note also the recently introduced Lasting Power of Attorney under the Mental Capacity Act. This important document allows us to choose beforehand, one(s) to act on our behalf if we are mentally incapacitated due to a stroke or dementia.

Lastly, legacy planning is about using the resources and experiences you have accumulated in life to make a lasting impression and impact on those you love and the causes you believe in.

Lastly, can you share and recommend what is your favourite book or books that have taught you about investing and unit trusts?

Why Stock Markets Will Always Rise by IFAST Financial co-founder Mr Mah Hong Meng shaped my thinking about investing. The book is written such that the average person on the street can understand. It gives three reasons why it is good to buy into the markets.

Firstly, global population will grow, thus revenues of companies will grow. As such, earnings should grow and share prices should grow with time. Second, the quality of consumption will increase. As people's disposable income increases, they will demand for better goods and services. About 20–30 years ago, Casio watches were very popular but nowadays people go for brands like Tag Heuer; people used to drive 700cc cars but, nowadays 1600cc and cars above 2000cc are common. All these will mean that the value of stocks and UTs should increase over time.

Lastly, the collective human spirit will always fight and endeavour to overcome challenges. When there is a crisis, governments will do their best to overcome the crisis and companies will also do their best to fight the down-times. We want our children to lead better lives than us. So overall, there will be more good years than bad years. So investing for the long term makes much sense, since there are more good years than bad years.

Resources

- **www.bloomberg.com.** *Bloomberg* is the leader in global business and financial news. It is updated in real time with 5,000 news articles daily.

- **www.valueline.com.** *Valueline* is an independent research and financial publishing firm based in New York. It has free research articles and commentaries for everyone to read to gain more insights.

- **www.fundsupermart.com.sg.** *Fundsupermart* is the online fund distribution arm of iFAST. It was started in 2000 and has arguably become the biggest market player for online UT distribution in Singapore. Their website also offers free research articles and Mr Wong Sui Jau's regular contributions can be read from this website.

- **www.investsmartsc.my.** Initiated by the Securities Commission of Malaysia to educate Malaysian investors and anyone who wants to invest in Malaysia asset classes (stocks, UTs, bonds, derivatives, warrants, etc.), this site has some good articles on Malaysia UT that I also used for this book.

- **www.investopedia.com.** This is the Wikipedia for investors to read articles and improve their financial understanding on financial terms and jargons, etc. They also have newsletters, tutorials, their own stock stimulator and FX trader.

- **www.fundsingapore.com.** This website is jointly produced by Investment Management Association of Singapore (IMAS) and Life Insurance Association of Singapore (LIA). Visitors to the website can scan and filter Singapore's UTs to set their search criteria (whether they want total return, consistent return, preservation or expenses). Since it is a Singapore UT website, visitors can also filter according to the CPF risk classification and whether the fund is approved for under the CPF investment scheme.

- **www.investinganswers.com.** This website has hundreds of free articles, tutorials and even basic financial calculators. They strive to present the articles in simple and as little jargon as possible to be an online financial dictionary and empower the readers to build and protect their wealth.

- **www.dollardex.com.** Started in 1999, *Dollardex* offers Singapore investor another choice other than Fundsupermart and Poems to invest in UTs. Readers can also use their investment analysis (like sell signal, heat map, etc.) There are also numerous articles and views on the markets that are regularly updated

- **www.poems.com.sg.** This is the other Singapore online UT platform mentioned. There is a ton of information on poems website as they also offer other financial products and services on top of UTs (stocks, futures, forex and gold, etc.). Readers only wanting to find out information on UTs may find this site too overloaded with information.

- **www.wsj.com.** The *Wall Street Journal* was first printed in 1889 and is a global leader and authority in reporting economics and finance news.

About the Author

Derek GUE is a financial strategist who advices on matters of a) income protection against premature death, critical illness, disability, etc.; b) savings for retirement; and c) investments, especially unit trusts. He also conducts public talks and lunchtime education talks at companies such as FedEx, Sembcorp Industries, and Wheelock Properties. He graduated from National University of Singapore in 2007 with a B.Sc (Real Estate) honours with a minor in Business Management. Find out more at www.derekgue.com.

www.ingramcontent.com/pod-product-compliance
Lightning Source LLC
Chambersburg PA
CBHW071216210326
41597CB00016B/1832